Joyous Expectation

Joyous Expectation

Journeying Through Advent with Mary

M. Jean Frisk

Pauline
BOOKS & MEDIA
Boston

Library of Congress Cataloging-in-Publication Data

Frisk, M. Jean.
 Joyous expectation : journeying through Advent with Mary / M. Jean
Frisk.
     p. cm.
 Includes bibliographical references.
 ISBN 0-8198-3982-5 (pbk.)
 1. Advent—Meditations. 2. Mary, Blessed Virgin, Saint. I. Title.
 BV40.F75 2005
 242'.332—dc22

                            2005004216

Cover art by Lea Maria Ravotti

Published by Pauline Books & Media, 50 Saint Pauls Avenue, Boston, MA 02130-3491. Printed in U.S.A.

www.pauline.org

Pauline Books & Media is the publishing house of the Daughters of St. Paul, an international congregation of women religious serving the Church with the communications media.

1 2 3 4 5 6 7 8 9   11 10 09 08 07 06 05

For all the Josephs who have loved Mary
and have taken her into their own homes
in Nazareth, Bethlehem, Egypt—everywhere—
that Christ can be born in hearts today.

Contents

Preface

To CELEBRATE CHRISTMAS is to journey in expectancy toward birthing and its aftermath. A woman waiting for childbirth is known to *nest*—to prepare her home from top to bottom: to gather, clean, weave, and wait. In her expectancy, Mary, too, waited and wondered.

Husbands prepare in their own way: providing, building, hammering, and pounding—pondering, too, this little stranger about to invade their territory. Joseph journeyed with Mary.

Some 2,000 years later, can we participate in the expectancy that Mary and Joseph felt? These pages are for those who would like to try.

Christmas today touches every life in some way. We know the challenges, joys, and tensions of the season. We can list all our *shoulds* until our conscience is burdened to breaking. But are all the *shoulds* the point?

Some of us want more. We want to accompany Mary and Joseph during that incarnational ninth month and those first birth days. But we are so busy, so burdened, so help-less. We ourselves are hungry and lonely. We mourn and we are poor. We count ourselves reviled, left out, strug-gling, wandering aimlessly from *The Early Morning Show* to *The Late Night Show.* Dry and empty, the depths of our souls feel the void of vibrancy. Or, are we driven to accom-plish—perhaps uncertain just what it is we ultimately want to accomplish? Does this in any way identify with the coming of the Messiah? What do we *really* want?

The northern hemisphere's December darkness brings long, perhaps lonely nights and millions of lights in the heavens and on the earth—sparkling, glittering, flashing lights echoing a star over a stable 2,000 years ago. If only we could run to the stable to witness there the glow centered on a manger—creation kneeling in prayer!

Is it love we want? Or does the very word evoke a bit-ter taste to our senses—hopes unfulfilled, relationships shattered? Is it love we want under the name of family, true caring for one another among colleagues, a world made fresh with springtime at the Christmas midnight hour?

Is it love we want?

We have heard countless Christmas legends. We long to be the little boy who takes Jesus for a ride in his red wagon, the little girl with nothing to give but roadside wild blossoms, the shepherd child playing the drum, the wise men who journey a long distance to bring the perfect gifts, the astonished midwife....

Do we want to give love?

Every year the pilgrimage starts anew with the coming of Advent. Some of us want more. Yes, we want to run to the stable, prepare it, be waiting for the holy couple to arrive—to be with them at the birthing, to listen, believe, pray. We hope each year that Christmas will be crowned by love—love received and love given.

Perhaps when we journey with Mary, she will share with us her love and its secrets.

How to Use This Book

Prepare

First, flip through these pages to look at the project boxes. You will find time-honored customs, devotions, and resources. Check the Saints, the notes, and the *All the Way to the Baptism of the Lord* sections for additional inspirational material.

Second, decide what faith-oriented symbols will be part of your home dècor this season. Objects can focus your reflection but can also distract you. For instance, will you weave an Advent wreath? Will you thoughtfully build up a crèche in your own creative setting? Do you have a prayer corner where you can peacefully reflect and pray? If you display your precious, fragile items where small children are present, will you also have touchable nativity figures, books, puzzles—things to involve their interaction with the Christmas mystery?

Third, set aside ten specific minutes a day to take this book in hand. Is early morning best for you or a 9 A.M.

coffee break once the kids are off to school? Are you retired and able to attend a daily church service? These reflections draw strongly on the liturgy. Or, if you work outside your home, is there any chance to stop at a place of prayer on the way home? Love is inventive in finding private time to be with the beloved. In any case, being consistent in the time frame will bring greater peace.

During the Advent section of this book the reflections are divided into three tasks: to ponder, to act, to pray.

You are invited to *ponder* as the Gospel writers tell us Mary did. Ponder sometimes in dialogue with Mary, other times with a saint of the day, then again within the liturgical focus of the season.

Then you are invited to *act* like Mary did after the Annunciation when she went in haste to help her cousin Elizabeth. *Action* doesn't necessarily mean projects and activities. It can also mean fostering an inner change in the way one approaches life. The way we think will ultimately determine what we do.

The reflection concludes with *prayer*, a prayer brief enough to remember and repeat again and again throughout the day. Sometimes taken from the liturgy, from holy writers, or the silence of the heart, the prayer is a jump-start for your own prayer of the heart.

The Christmas and Epiphany sections of the book offer suggestions on how to continue and sustain a sense of celebration. The pattern of pondering, acting, and praying now melts into the routine of everyday life.

Finally, it is essential to set your priorities for how *you* want to celebrate the seasons. Make a plan. Choose the prism for your vision. You probably know dozens of Advent and Christmas customs—religious and secular—from every nation on earth, and books about them abound. This season is like turning a child's kaleidoscope of brightly colored glass to form pattern after pattern of many-faceted stars. Yet each star, regardless of its number of rays, has its focal point, its golden center that unites the pattern: to celebrate the coming of Jesus. As long as he remains the focal point, everything will harmoniously flow together. To focus your own strength and time, you many want to drop those things and activities that purposely exclude him.

For young families the focus could be a grand celebration of Jesus' birthday. For those who are alone—and they are many—the focus could be that final coming when we will meet Jesus face to face. Select your focus, but by all means plan to celebrate!

Foster Expectation

Wreaths and trees, candles, cakes, and cookies;
Gifts and myths, wassail, fine wine, and holly;
Visits and pageants, cards, e-mails, and *Las Posadas*;

Jesse tree, *Missa de Gallo*, red, green, and mistletoe;
"O" Antiphons and carols, Immaculata, Guadalupe,
building a crèche piece by piece;
Shepherds and kings, Barbara, Nicholas, and Lucy;
Donkeys and oxen, little lambs, incense, and gold;
Angels, dreams, innkeepers, cousins, and friends;
Chocolates, candy canes, garland, and glitter.

All of these and much more weave the fabric of
Christmas. Like every weaving, the back side can be a
mess of tangles and tied knots—symbol of our hectic
lives. Keeping your regularly set ten minutes of pondering and prayer will help you to turn over the masterpiece
and focus on the things of God that are important to you.
As the Amish make their prized quilts with an intention-
al flaw, a flaw must be woven in to remind us that only
God is perfect. When Jesus took flesh, he came to the
back side of things. The purpose of Christmas is to meet
him, imitate him, love him at the back side and the deep
inside of everything.

When you set aside your ten minutes treat them as if
they were the first of for ever. Not everything will go as
planned, but remember, masters of the spiritual life recom-
mend that we reserve the final moments in the evening to
reflect on how we have walked with God during the day.
Those last thoughts echo through the night and wake with
us to set the tone of the new day. Foster gentle, grateful, lov-

ing expectancy that tomorrow your purpose is to seek, to find, and to serve the little child who is the Messiah. Start over tomorrow. Live as Mary lived. Pray as Mary prayed.

She listened:

"And of his kingdom there will be no end" (Lk 1:33).

She responded:

"Here am I, the servant of the Lord,
let it be with me according to your word" (Lk 1:38).

First Week of Advent

We believe and confess that Jesus of Nazareth,
born a Jew of a daughter of Israel at Bethlehem
at the time of King Herod the Great and the emperor
    Caesar Augustus,
a carpenter by trade,
who died crucified in Jerusalem under the procurator
    Pontius Pilate
during the reign of the emperor Tiberius,
is the eternal Son of God made man.

(*Catechism of the Catholic Church*, no. 423)

Sunday

of the First Week of Advent

Ponder

THE MARKING OF TIME and its turning is a remarkably human thing. Inexorably, the minutes and hours move forward and never reverse. Yet the discovery of cycles of years connotes its own hope. We may begin anew, make resolutions, hope that love will flourish again.

For Christian churches the message of Jesus Christ is condensed in a year's cycle—celebrated from glory to glory: his coming, his ministry, his death, his resurrection, and his future coming.

Advent begins a new year. Yes, Jesus came and he will come again. He will be with us and take us home. Till then our life is a pilgrimage. Each Advent we may start once more to live with him and in him. We have the option to become a testimony of his loving redemption, to share in it through who we are and what we do, and finally to recall our own eternal destiny.

Advent Wreath

A wreath is a ring; a ring has no end. Advent wreaths are usually made of evergreens to remind us of life everlasting—ultimately our lives will have no end. Four candles mark the  weeks. The candles are often purple (for sorrow and penitent waiting) and pink for the third week (to rejoice for the Lord is near), but in some countries red, gold, and natural honeycomb wax are used to symbolize the precious busyness of our lives preparing for the coming of the King.

Select your own symbols. Make them meaningful for you. Light the first candle today. Pray with the Church:

Lord God,
your Church joyfully awaits the coming of its
    Savior,
who enlightens our hearts
and dispels the darkness of ignorance and sin.

Pour forth your blessings upon us
as we light the candles of this wreath;
may their light reflect the splendor of Christ,
who is Lord, for ever and ever. Amen.

(Taken from the *Book of Blessings*, nos. 1509—1540)

But *how* can we live with him, love him, focus on him, learn from him, sit at his feet, bake bread for him to break? We look to those who did. We hope to learn from them the answer to *how*.

*M*ary of Nazareth, draw me to your company. Tell me the stories of your Son, the memories of your people. This first Sunday of Advent is a reminder of Jesus' coming at the end of time. It is said that you are a bridge across time: daughter of Israel, bearer of the Messiah. You embody the expectation of both covenants: the hunger for his saving power to set things right in this world and the longing for eternal fulfillment, at last to be content, happy, at peace. Mary, let me learn from you.

Act

Today, foster the desire to seek and find Jesus.

Pray

Lord, come! Let me find you; let me see you face to face.

Monday

of the First Week of Advent

Ponder

WE SET OUR OWN VALUES for the holidays. So does the commercial world. We admittedly rejoice when the commentators tell us *sales are up*. A nation's prosperity benefits its people.

The Church also gives us a prism for Advent. This week the lens is the prophet Isaiah. He speaks of the Lord's house to be established, all nations streaming toward it.

Many peoples shall come and say,
"Come, let us go up to the mountain of the LORD...
that he may teach us his ways
 and that we may walk in his paths" (Is 2:3).

Mary of the Chosen People surely knew this. What did she think when she knew God's promise, but her nation was subject to another's rule? As we journey with her, we wonder what it was like for her in her ninth month. By this time she had prepared what she needed for her baby's arrival. Old stories tell us she was a weaver of fine linen. Her child would have the best. Joseph, a carpenter by trade, would have made the dwelling ready in his own way—crafting the finest cradle ever. They were ready.

We, too, plan our Christmas to be the finest and best ever.

According to Luke's account, the couple had to set aside their plans and preparations. They left Nazareth and traveled about 110 miles southeast through rugged, mountainous, desert terrain to Bethlehem, a city five miles south of Jerusalem.

Why didn't Joseph leave Mary at home? Must a whole family be displaced in the name of ancient roots or another's prosperity? Must one nation have such power over another—for whatever reason? The sacred word doesn't tell us. It was, after all, Joseph's task to keep her close, to protect her and this child. Or, could it be that Mary insisted on going along?

→ ✾ ←

*M*ary, Bethlehem was a long way from home for you—walking, donkey back, desert heat and cold, hills and valleys. On the journey, did you recall Isaiah's promise of peace and wonder if your child was the One, the only One, who could establish it? In the desert did you remember that the Lord's glory would be *"a shade by day from the heat, and a refuge and shelter from the storm and rain"* (Is 4:6)?

One thing is certain: The child would be born in David's city—Bethlehem, House of Bread. Jesus would later tell us: *"I tell you, many will come from east and west and will eat with Abraham and Isaac and Jacob in the kingdom of heaven"* (Mt 8:11). He himself would become the bread for the banquet.

Act

Today, use the time going from one place to another to wonder as Mary wondered. Think of gifts you will give and receive. Often each gift has parts and packaging. From beginning to end, from raw materials to assembly, think of the hands, from all the nations, that made your gifts. Pray for the makers of the gifts you intend to give and those you will receive.

Pray

Lord our God, help us to prepare for the coming of Christ your Son. May he find us waiting, eager in joyful prayer.

(From the Opening Prayer of today's Mass)

Tuesday

of the First Week of Advent

Ponder

ISAIAH'S ELEVENTH CHAPTER DESCRIBES the perfect king who will rise up to rule the peoples. The verses give us the stuff of wonderful Christmas legends and depictions:

A shoot shall come out from the stump of Jesse,
   and a branch shall grow out of his roots.
The spirit of the LORD shall rest on him,
   the spirit of wisdom and understanding,
   the spirit of counsel and might....
...he shall judge the poor,
   and decide with equity for the meek of the earth....
They will not hurt or destroy on all my holy mountain;
for the earth will be full of the knowledge of the LORD...
The wolf shall live with the lamb,
   the leopard shall lie down with the kid,
the calf and the lion and the fatling together,
   and a little child shall lead them (Is 11:1–2, 4, 9, 6).

Jesse Tree

If you have time, make a Jesse tree. The tree traces Jesus' ancestry through brief Scripture readings, one for each day of Advent. Children make or color symbols to represent the passages being read. Hang them like ornaments on a small tree or  attach them to a calendar. Talk about the symbols.

Some resources:

Jesse Tree Kit: An Advent Project for Family, Class-room or Parish, written and illustrated by Lynn M. Simms and Betsy Walker, Pauline Books & Media.

Text & symbols *(general)*:
www.geocities.com/Heartland/7202/advent.html

Craft *(children)*:
http://www.domestic-church.com/index.dir/ index_articles.htm

Mary Page meditation *(adult)*:
www.udayton.edu/mary/meditations/jessetree.html

Heart-warming Christmas stories tell of wonderful things happening when Mary rides with Joseph at the lead. Scoundrels grow gentle, thieves back off, lions run. Are we permitted such fantastic imaginings and storytelling? Jesus prays in Luke's Gospel: *"I thank you, Father, Lord of heaven and earth, because you have hidden these things from the wise and the intelligent and have revealed them to infants; yes, Father, for such was your gracious will"* (Lk 10:21).

*M*ary, Christmas and its seasons are about the child you bear. It's also about seeing the world fresh and new with the eyes of a child—trusting, believing in goodness, undismayed to see the lion and lamb at play.

Is there something I can do to become more like a child? Jesus tells me: *"Truly I tell you, unless you change and become like children, you will never enter the kingdom of heaven. Whoever becomes humble like this child is the greatest in the kingdom of heaven. Whoever welcomes one such child in my name welcomes me"* (Mt 18:3–4).

Act

Ponder children today. Find Jesus in their faces. Find some way to love a child.

Pray

Ask for the grace to walk humbly with our God as we know his humble servant, Mary, did.

Wednesday

of the First Week of Advent

Ponder

A FESTIVE MEAL HAS A CERTAIN QUALITY that bonds hearts. In our culture, Advent is about parties and baking, giving and taking. What an honor to receive an invitation; what joy to host the festival!

The Church's message today through Isaiah tells how the Lord

> *"will make for all peoples*
> *a feast of rich food, a feast of well-aged wines, ...*
> *And he will destroy on this mountain*
> *the shroud that is cast over all peoples,*
> *the sheet that is spread over all nations;*
> *he will swallow up death forever.*
> *Then the Lord GOD will wipe away the tears from all*
> *   faces" (Is 25:6–8).*

This was the promise; in Jesus it was fulfilled. The Gospel of Matthew tells us today how Jesus' heart was

*Christmas Family Gatherings
by Donata Maggipinto*
(Chronicle Books, 2003)

Recipes and ideas for celebrating with people you love.
www.chroniclebooks.com

moved with pity for the people. He fed them and food
abounded for all.

We hear it time and again. We *know* it in the core of our
being. If we would learn to share, to really care, there would
be enough for all.

Does this refer to material goods alone? Sharing, caring
is first of all a deep inner awareness of *others.* This takes
place in the communicating silence of prayer. A person
wrapped in self finds it difficult to pray. Like a finely
adorned package, the selfish person, hoarding all for his or
her own pleasure, is empty when unwrapped.

Mary's final words in Scripture are a prayer and a directive. She has accepted an invitation to a wedding feast.
Amidst the festivities she observes quietly the pending
embarrassment of the family. Her prayer is simple: *They have
no wine.* She knows the Lord's goodness and his power. Her
directive is just as simple: *"Do whatever he tells you"* (Jn 2:5).

*M*ary, how many dinners did you prepare? Did you plan celebrations for your child when he was little? Did you host parties, too? What about family and friends? Some traditions say that Joseph had grown children by another marriage. If it is true, did the whole clan descend upon you with spouses and children and grandchildren? How did you handle the party, Mary? What choice foods and rich wines did you enjoy? What menu did you plan? Mary, I'm a bit desperate; will you lend me your recipe for happy family gatherings?

Act

Observe quietly today: Is there some way to reach out, to extend an invitation, to care, to share?

Pray

Lord our God, grant that we may be ready to receive Christ when he comes in glory and to share in the banquet of heaven.

(From the Opening Prayer of today's Mass)

Thursday

of the First Week of Advent

Ponder

ISAIAH'S MESSAGE TODAY asks us to *"trust in the Lord for ever, for in the Lord GOD you have an everlasting rock"* (26:4). And how simple is the opening prayer of Mass: *Father, we need your help.*

Did such simple prayers well up in the hearts of Joseph and Mary on the journey to Bethlehem? Even in the intimacy with her unborn child—God within her—Mary needed help. God provided. She was not alone; Joseph, just and loyal, stayed close to her. Mary belonged in Joseph's care by the legal arrangement of the engagement contract, as was the custom of the time. She may even have lived in his home during part of the engagement to learn the ways of his household. Scripture doesn't tell us so, but ancient customs indicate it may have been so.

Surely Mary sang praise to God for Joseph! He stood with her though this was not his child. How kind and strong the Scriptures depict him!

*M*ary, spiritual writers tell us that God's plan sheltered you and your divine Son in a wondrous way. After the angel's announcement you hurried off to help your cousin Elizabeth. You stayed there three months. Some writers think Joseph brought you to Elizabeth. Others believe he discovered you with child when you returned. In any case, you and Joseph traveled the road to Bethlehem, and if the story is rightly told, you went from there to Egypt before finally going home to Nazareth. By that time, in that era, the hometown would hardly have kept track of months or even years. In this way, Mary, God protected you and your child from discrimination based on doubt about his birth.

Actually, the sequence of the biography doesn't really matter. God's revelation matters.

In the liturgy today, Jesus talks about the wise man who built his house on solid rock. The people who listen to his word and keep it are the Josephs and the Marys—then and of every age—who are faithful, strong, loving.

Blossoms in Winter

In third-century Rome, a woman named Barbara, daughter of Dioscorus, became Christian. Her father handed her over to the authorities and personally executed her, as Roman law allowed the heads of households to do. The legend says that Barbara found a branch of a cherry tree in her prison tower, shared her water with it, and that it blossomed just before she died, symbol of her youth and beauty given to Christ. Barbara's liturgical memorial was formerly celebrated by the universal Church on December 4.

In German tradition branches of the cherry tree (forsythia work well, too) are cut early in December. By Christmas the blossoms will bring joy to the Christ Child where they decorate his crèche.

Act

Today, look at life, yours and your neighbor's. How often did our gracious God turn apparent misfortune into richest blessings!

Pray

As we serve you now, accept our offering and sustain us with your promise of eternal life.

(From the Prayer Over the Gifts of today's Mass)

Friday

of the First Week of Advent

Ponder

FRIDAY! IT IS AN EXHAUSTING DAY. We are glad for it and hope that nothing will disturb the coming weekend. True! Quiet and prayer may be more fearsome than pushy crowds and TV violence. Do I have the courage to take some time to sit still and try to touch God in my silence? Perhaps I am afraid to listen to what my own inner voice has to say, anxious that I will receive no answer. So, instead, I cover it with other noises. But Friday is the day of the Lord's death. If today is a first Friday, this brings to mind the Catholic tradition to tenderly recall his loving, Sacred Heart. At least I could try to spend some time recalling his love. He may indeed answer me!

Isaiah tells us today that when the Holy One of Israel comes, miracles will take place: forests will blossom, fields will be fruitful, the deaf will hear, the blind will see, the people who are unhappy will now find new joy, and the needy will rejoice (cf. Is 29:17–20).

It sounds too good to be true, but when Jesus went throughout the land doing good, he performed such mighty deeds. Yet he didn't hoard those acts of goodness as his own power. He shared these powers with his disciples, with the saints, and now he shares them with us.

Our actions may not be as miraculously spectacular as Jesus' actions. Nonetheless, every act of kindness, every meal on the table, every drop of sweat on the brow, and every burden of the day well-mastered are little miracles, a share in building the kingdom Jesus came to establish in the land of the living, a kingdom that will have no end.

*M*ary, the time when life went on as usual in your household is called the hidden life. So little is known about your life with the Lord, but then again, if I think about it, I know what daily life is all about—the little and big things, the mundane routine, paying bills, washing clothes, shopping for groceries, the aches and pains, the joys and celebrations. Your life was not so different from mine. Maybe that is why the changing seasons and festivals mean so much to me.

Willard F. Jabusch's text and its Slovakian folk melody remind me of your hidden life:

See how the Virgin waits for him;
Mary in wonder waits for him.
Shake off your slumber; come all full of wonder.
    Jesus is coming as the Prince of Peace.

    Gently she hears the distant breeze
    swaying the silver olive trees.
    What is she thinking as the sun is sinking
    waiting the birthday of her firstborn Son?

Now a new pattern on the loom;
now a new presence in the room.
Waking or sleeping, all her love she's keeping,
waiting the coming of the Son of God.[1]

Can I find time for quiet reflection this Friday evening,
time to think of the *new presence in the room*? The God of life
is indeed always with me even if I fail to recognize his presence. Can I find time to focus on priorities?

Act

Join the Church today in quietly praying for those
whose hearts are wide enough to follow Jesus fully into
priestly ministry and the consecrated life, those who
are willing to allow their hearts to bleed and break by

---

1. Willard F. Jabusch, "See How the Virgin Waits for Him," Oregon
Catholic Press.

serving him in us. Invite someone to join you in this intention.

Pray

Jesus, shake off my slumber, come all full of wonder, come as the Prince of Peace.

Saturday

of the First Week of Advent

Ponder

Is this the day the lights go on the porch and the wreath is hung on the door? The first cards are arriving. Have I begun mine? Shall I save that for Sunday, or shall I write at all? E-mail might do the trick. But I have packages to send, and what was that deadline? What about the tree? Customs differ. But, yes, definitely a tree.

Do you sense my panic?

Isaiah tells us today that the Lord will graciously hear me when I cry out. *"As soon as he hears he will answer you. The LORD will give you the bread you need and the water for which you thirst"* (30:19–20 NAB). But that doesn't mean his answer will be *my* wish and will! Nonetheless, I have the promise—he *will* answer, but he places some conditions: he has to hear my cry. I must trust he can work miracles.

True, the Scriptures tell me that the Lord knows my inmost thoughts. He knows my need before I can express it.

Still, he waits for my wanting. This is the mystery of my freedom.

Christmas Trees

Ace Collins tells us that the custom of decorating evergreen trees during the Advent season to anticipate Christmas has been widely practiced for only about two centuries. The custom of using evergreen branches as a Christian symbol to express everlasting life and hope can be traced back more than a thousand years. Later, says Collins, "Legend has it that Martin Luther was walking home on a dark December evening when he was struck by the beauty of the starlight coming through the branches of the many fir trees in the woods around his home." Luther brought a tree into his home and tried to duplicate the effect by placing little candles on the branches. "Luther taught his friends and family that the tree represented the everlasting love of God.... The candlelight represented the hope that Christ brought to the world through his birth and resurrection."

(Ace Collins, *Stories Behind the Great Traditions of Christmas* [Grand Rapids: Zondervan, 2003], pp. 70f.).

Mary, at the Annunciation—spiritual writers tell us—all creation held its breath waiting for your answer. The Lord God himself waited for your wanting. That realization overwhelms me! That God would wait for the freely given answer of a young girl!

Tradition tells me that Jewish girls married and bore children at a very young age. Some persons may overlook your freedom to accept or refuse, so explicitly stated in Luke's account. If his narrative is true, and I believe it is, then, in spite of your youth, you held wisdom beyond your years. You pondered, you questioned, and you answered in reflective, calm freedom. Love was the measure.

On Saturday, traditionally called Mary's day, liturgies are dedicated in your honor and you are worthy of honor, for you freely became the Christ-bearer and Christ-bringer, his constant associate and companion in all things.

Act

Today, recall Mary's role in salvation history. Think about receiving the Eucharist at the Sunday liturgy. To receive the Body of Christ is to be, like Mary, a bearer of Christ. Like Mary, we can walk through our world bringing his spirit, his message, above all, his love.

Christmas Crèche

Some churches and homes slowly erect the Nativity scene week by week. Many begin by using an Annunciation scene, and then replacing it piece by piece  with figures of angels, people, animals, and nature that are found at the manger. Some crèches depict everyday life and society as it was then—shepherds and innkeepers and all who gathered in Bethlehem—but reflect what society is today—bakers, teachers, children—who represent every imaginable profession and way of life. A crèche brings out cultural imagination at its best.

Pray

Mary, let us reflect your image and walk through life entirely like you: strong and noble, simple and kind, spreading love and peace and joy. In us go through our times and make them ready for Christ.[2]

---

2. Joseph Kentenich, "Hymn of the Instruments," in *Heavenwards: Prayers Written in Dachau* (Waukesha, WI: Schoenstatt Press, 1992).

Second Week of Advent

The coming of God's Son to earth is an event of such immensity that God willed to prepare for it over centuries. He makes everything converge on Christ: all the rituals and sacrifices, figures and symbols of the "First Covenant" (Heb 9:15)....

St. John the Baptist is the Lord's immediate precursor or forerunner, sent to prepare his way.... He inaugurates the Gospel, already from his mother's womb welcomes the coming of Christ, and rejoices in being "the friend of the bridegroom," whom he points out as "the Lamb of God, who takes away the sin of the world."

(*Catechism of the Catholic Church*, nos. 522–523)

Sunday

of the Second Week of Advent

Ponder

THE SECOND CANDLE OF THE WREATH burns brightly. As we set our priorities and proceed with our plans, we see this season through the prism of Jesus. Probably the back side of the masterpiece looks jumbled. But today we can begin again. By all means celebrate!

Prophet after prophet announced the coming of the Messiah to Israel. The first reading in Cycle C for the second Sunday of Advent is from the prophet Baruch. In wonderful poetry, he speaks of forests and fragrant trees overshadowing Israel

"...at God's command.
For God will lead Israel with joy, in the light of his glory,
with the mercy and righteousness that come from him" (5:9).
Christmas trees recall that joy.

The second reading, from Paul's letter to the Philippians, overflows with tenderness, strength, and longing.

Could anyone write a better Christmas message? *"I thank my God every time I remember you, constantly praying with joy in every one of my prayers for all of you, because of your sharing in the gospel from the first day until now.... And this is my prayer, that your love may overflow more and more with knowledge and full insight to help you to determine what is best, so that on the day of Christ you may be pure and blameless"* (Phil 1:3–5, 9–10), filled with the fruits of justice and joy.

The liturgy anticipates the child. Joy waits to burst everywhere. It is announced by John, son of Zechariah and Elizabeth, cousin of Mary, the Mother of Jesus. John travels throughout the Jordan area *"proclaiming a baptism of repentance for the forgiveness of sins"* (Lk 3:3).

We might think of John as an angry young man wearing hairy camel skins, eating locusts and honey, and wildly shouting warnings in the desert. Angry? Probably not! Even the gentlest voice resounds in the desert. To banish deceit and sin is a wonderfully happy thing. When we read Luke we discover a man who knew joy even in his mother's womb! To Mary, who has come to help her, Elizabeth says, *"And why has this happened to me, that the mother of my Lord comes to me? For as soon as I heard the sound of your greeting, the child in my womb leapt for joy"* (Lk 1:43–44).

*M*ary, years later, did you hear John's challenge to prepare for the Lord's coming? Did you remember when your babies met for the first time? And if John leapt for joy, what did you feel? What was it like to be filled with the presence of God day and night, fully filled with love? Will I ever know?

Act

Today, take quiet time to reflect on the symbols of God's presence among the people of the first covenant. Yet, is there anything to compare with God's presence in Mary?

Pray

God of power and mercy, open our hearts in welcome. Remove the things that hinder us from receiving Christ with joy.

(From the Opening Prayer of today's Mass)

Monday

of the Second Week of Advent

Ponder

THE LITURGY TODAY BRINGS US to the mysterious world of Jesus' power to heal. The reading from Isaiah tells us that feeble hands and weak knees will be strengthened. God will come and save hearts filled with fear, and *"the lame shall leap like a deer"* (35:6).

The Gospel shows how Jesus did these things in Luke's wonderful story of the men who lowered a paralyzed man on a stretcher through the roof. Luke writes, *"When he saw their faith, he said, 'Friend, your sins are forgiven you'"* (5:20). Perhaps Jesus had been teaching about sin. Whatever the case, those listening got upset, to say the least. God alone can forgive sin! We know the rest of the story: The man got up, picked up his cot himself, and went home.

Look at the text again. A man needs help. It took the *faith* of several friends to aid him, to get him to Jesus. The healer sees the deeper need; body and soul both require healing—the health of one affects the other.

The Church invites us to find time during Advent to seek spiritual health through the forgiveness of sins. We see it in the opening prayer for today: "Lord, free us from our sins and make us whole." Charles Dickens tells it well when he has dear old Scrooge recognize who he really is— with the help of old friends, of course, be they in heaven, hell, or on earth! Scrooge does change, and the plight of Tiny Tim finally turns his heart. Even the most selfish can choose to love.

*J*esus, when you teach the two commandments—love of God and love of neighbor—you make it clear that the greatest sins spring from my lack of love. They crop up in my self-centeredness and selfishness, my lack of caring about God and others. I look inward—not to search for the face of God but to make self the center of my circling. Advent gives me an opportunity to make all things new.

Act

Today, talk with Mary about yourself. Find an image of her where she looks at you face to face. Ask her to be that friend who lets you see where selfishness has taken a strangle-hold on your life. Think of Mary with Jesus in the texts and images of Scripture. In them, she gives examples of someone who knows how to care no matter what the journey or the personal cost.

Pray

Mary, help me do my best to be rid of sin, self-centered-ness, and selfishness so that Christmas will shine.

Christmas Cards

In *Stories Behind the Great Traditions of Christmas*, 2003, Ace Collins tells us that cards for Christmas were first published in England in 1843. The center  panel of the first card depicted a happy family and friends celebrating, but the two outer panels of the threefold showed people helping the poor who needed food and clothing. It does us good to remember.

Tuesday

of the Second Week of Advent

Ponder

A CRÈCHE IN THE EXHIBITS of The Marian Library/ International Marian Research Institute in Dayton, Ohio, has a large flock of sheep gathered around the stable. Sheep stand everywhere.

It reminds me of today's Gospel when Jesus tells the story of the shepherd leaving the ninety-nine to search for the one who strayed. The shepherd didn't lose the lamb; it strayed away. The shepherd's profit is in the ninety-nine, not in the one. But the shepherd cares on a level that doesn't count utility and profit. *"So it is not the will of your Father in heaven that one of these little ones should be lost"* (Mt 18:14).

The text from Isaiah powerfully says that God asks us to speak tenderly to Jerusalem, to comfort his people, but also to courageously cry out to the cities:

"Here is your God....
He will feed his flock like a shepherd;
he will gather the lambs in his arms,
and carry them in his bosom,
and gently lead the mother sheep" (40:9–11).

Mary's name has been interpreted since early Christian centuries, and it has at least seventy meanings. As the *Dictionary of Mary* states: "The name has the form *Myriam* in the Hebrew Old Testament and *Maryam* in the Aramaic, *Mariam* in the Greek translation of the Old Testament, and *Maria* in the Greek New Testament."[3] Modern philology traces the name to the Egyptian *mara* (satiated, fat, or corpulent—"in accord with Oriental feminine esthetic, *beautiful*"), or the Egyptian *mari* (loved). A third philological opinion is that it is *mrym,* an ancient Canaanite word akin to Hebrew (high, lofty, exalted, august, *the Exalted One* or *the Sublime One*).

Devotion to Mary also seeks symbolic meaning for her name. Among the symbols the poetic opinion holds that her name means *ewe,* or mother sheep. When we speak of Jesus as the Lamb of God, we may think of his Mother as the ewe who gives him birth.

How fitting then to think of Isaiah's affirmation that God leads the ewes, the mothers, with care. In spite of

---

3. *Dictionary of Mary,* various authors (New York: Catholic Book Publishing Co., 1991).

immense hardships, in her pregnancy God led Mary with care, protecting her during all her journeys. At his death, Jesus looked at her and provided for her—not only sheltering her, but giving her the task to continue being Mother for all times.

*M*ary, when only the tangles and knots of the masterpiece show, do I know that God holds me in his arms, caring tenderly? Do I know that part of his caring is to entrust me with the task to care for others? Mary, even in the bitterness of tears and death, your life shows me that the best possible way to overcome sorrow and distress is to care for others—even if only by smiling at the check-out counter.

Act

Make it a point to find and respond to Christ's face in the suffering of others—at the gas pump, in the parking lot, wherever harried people need a kindly smile.

Pray

Lord, we are nothing without you. As you sustain us with your mercy, receive our prayers and offerings. We ask this through Christ our Lord.

(From the Prayer Over the Gifts of today's Mass)

Wednesday

of the Second Week of Advent

Ponder

ALL-POWERFUL FATHER,
we await the healing power of Christ your Son.
Let us not be discouraged by our weaknesses
as we prepare for his coming.
Keep us steadfast in your love.

(Opening Prayer of Mass)

How often we have heard it said: We are our own worst enemy. I've noticed that I often detest in others the flaws that mark me as well. What to do about it? Admit it. Don't be shocked by it. Try again. Above all, don't say: So what; I can't change.

In today's Gospel, Jesus tells us to put on his harness and learn from him—he compares himself to a beast of burden or a slave harnessed at the master's bidding, for he is meek and has a humble heart. Then Jesus promises that we will find rest for ourselves if we do these things. If we master life's trials *his* way, we will find them light and easy.

*M*ary, an old Advent song, probably written by a Benedictine monk in an abbey near the Matthias Church in Trier, Germany, speaks of you as the Christ-bearer. Miracles happen when you pass by with his life within you.

The Matthias Church has a side chapel with a painting of you beautifully dressed as you probably never were. You have on a dark blue brocade dress laced in pearls. You wear a lovely, simple pearl crown that hints of a cross. Your gaze shows that you are lost in thought, and a soft smile plays on your lips. The secret of the image lies in your expectancy. Your hands gently pull the folds of your garment to fullness under your heart. Jesus is present within you.

Mary, through baptism Christ's life is mine. Through his sacraments he dwells in me. Couldn't wonderful things happen when we two draw near?

Maria walks amid the thorn,
*Kyrie eleison!**
Maria walks amid the thorn

---

* *Kyrie eleison*—Greek for Lord, have mercy.

which seven years no leaf had born.
Jesus et Maria.**

> What 'neath her heart does Mary bear?
> *Kyrie eleison!*
> A little child does Mary bear,
> beneath her heart he nestles there.
> *Jesus et Maria.*

And as the two are passing near,
Kyrie eleison!
Lo, roses on the thorn appear;
Lo, roses on the thorn appear!
Jesus et Maria.

(Geistliche Volkslieder, 1850)

Act

*Be aware that Christ dwells in you—or desires to.
What can you do to give him a worthy dwelling?*

Pray

Jesus, make the dry thorns of my heart and life manifest roses for others.

** *Jesus et Maria*—Latin for Jesus and Mary.

Thursday

of the Second Week of Advent

Ponder

IN ISAIAH'S POETRY, the Lord calls Jacob a worm and Israel a maggot (41:14). Of course, some translations soften it a little by using the word *insect*. The *King James* version just says *ye men of Israel*. In any case, that name-calling jolts us, especially at 7 A.M. Mass. Would we be able to take it if the Lord faced us squarely with our reality?

The text goes on to tell us that the Lord will help even worms and maggots; the promises of prosperity, fertile, fruitful lands, and precious forests continue—in fact, mightily! *"You shall rejoice in the LORD; in the Holy One of Israel you shall glory"* (Is 41:16). The point of the reading: The wonderful things happening to Israel will ultimately be *God's* doing, not ours. *"The hand of the LORD has done this, the Holy One of Israel has created it"* (Is 41:20).

In Matthew's Gospel, Jesus talks to the crowds. Some support him; others object to everything he says and does.

He praises the greatness of his cousin, John the Baptist. At the same time, Jesus tells us that the least in the Father's kingdom is greater than John.

In *A Guide to the Eucharist and Hours*, Kevin W. Irwin unravels these texts wonderfully. He says that John is a "model of unprecedented self-effacement before God." John knows his importance, but he "humbly stands aside when the Lord comes." Irwin goes on, "John, this last and specially chosen prophet, leads us by word and example to realize that we too must be self-effacing before the Lord."

Isn't it true: We hope people will like what we did for them, be grateful for our efforts, say "thank you" for the hot chocolate and cookies.... Obviously, we've done the deed for ourselves, if we expect thanks.

Irwin's final comments say it all:

> John's example functions as a most important Advent model for us, especially as we prepare for the coming holidays. There are cards to send, gifts to purchase, food to prepare, family to please, and neighbors to greet. But, in all this, we ought to remember why we do it—out of love for others and to spread the peace of Christ, the true gift of Christmas. We are to incarnate Jesus' love in our daily lives among those we love and especially among those who do not love us.[4]

4. Kevin W. Irwin, *A Guide to the Eucharist and Hours: Advent and Christmas* (New York: Pueblo Publishing Company, 1986), p. 77.

Mary, I can't quite imagine that you pouted when your Son ran in, grabbed a cookie, and ran off to play with his friends. Well, I can't imagine that he forgot to say thank you either. Are you smiling? Isn't this the normal backside of every weaving? Help me not to take myself too seriously!

Act

Today, do what you do for the doing of it and for the Lord—not for the thanks you will or won't receive. That's the stuff of saints!

Pray

Jesus, teach me to pray like Isaiah: "The hand of the Lord has done this, the Holy One of Israel has created it." (41:20).

Friday

of the Second Week of Advent

Ponder

THE WINTER SOLSTICE IS APPROACHING. It's four in the afternoon in my northern home, but the sun has dipped below the horizon. The workweek counts down. Just about three more weeks till the year ends. Will my prism still catch and spill rainbows across the ceiling, bright signs of hope and joy?

Maybe at the beginning of this weekend I will find time to read a Christmas story or two, light a candle, pull out those forgotten beads, truly add prayer to my Christmas gifts....

The late Bishop Kenneth Untener of Saginaw, Michigan, used to put together *The Little Blue Advent Book* for Advent each year. The 2003 edition contains this powerful reflection for the lonely:

Why am I doing this?

She lived alone, as so many do. And she felt it especially at Christmas, as so many do.

Decorating her Christmas tree, she began to argue with herself, an argument she'd had several times before in these days before Christmas. "Why am I doing this? No one will see it, and I don't need it."

Then she heard herself say, "You *have* to do this. Not so that others will see it, but to remind yourself that the hope is real—not just words or a dream. It's real. Jesus really did come. And so you really have a tree, and you decorate it, and you buy real gifts, and you go to Midnight Mass, and you have a real Christmas dinner. This is how you keep the hope alive and real."[6]

(Bishop Kenneth E. Untener, *Little Blue Advent Book*, Diocese of Saginaw, 2003, www.saginaw.org/advent/lbb_info.htm.)

Act

Today, take quiet time to reflect on the final coming of Jesus, the moment he will call you home, when he will take you across the threshold to the Father's eternal Christmas celebration. Be ready to embrace those you loved and who loved you, with Mary and all the saints.

Crib Straws

Families with children may enjoy this symbolic way of preparing for Christmas. Cover a container, such as a shoebox, with decorative wrapping, or use plain paper with nativity cut-outs or symbols. Each day family members place pieces of straw or shredded paper in the box. Each piece represents a good deed or unselfish act done that day. On Christmas Eve, that "straw" is placed in the manger and becomes the bed for Baby Jesus.

Pray

Rejoice, Mary, the Lord is with you! Blessed are you among women and blessed is the fruit of your womb, Jesus. Holy Mary, Mother of God, pray for us sinners, now and at the hour of our death. Amen.

Saturday

of the Second Week of Advent

Ponder

THE OLD TESTAMENT READING praises Elijah, the courageous prophet who defied King Ahab and his scheming wife Jezebel, who killed the Lord's prophets and worshiped idols (see 1 Kgs 16:29–21:29). The text from Sirach says that Elijah was destined *"to put an end to wrath, to turn back the hearts of fathers toward their sons"* (48:10). Especially moving is the blessing for those who fall asleep in Elijah's friendship.

In the Gospel, the disciples ask Jesus about Elijah. The answer Jesus gives makes them aware that John the Baptist has fulfilled Elijah's role. In this serious moment, Jesus also tells them that he will suffer.

Some images of Mary show the Christ Child laid out on her lap like Michelangelo's *Pieta.* Puerto Rico's *Divina Providentia*—Our Lady of Divine Providence—is one such image. This child—like every child—is born to die.

Las Posadas—*Shelter Seeking*

An Article from Mary Page

Q: Why does a statue or image of the Blessed Virgin Mary go from home to home in some communities?

A: The origin of this custom is the so-called shelter seeking of the Holy Family on their way to Bethlehem. They seek a shelter where they can stay for the night and where Mary can give birth to Jesus. From the recollection of this event grew the medieval "Frauen-tragen" (carrying of Our Lady) in Germany, and later the so-called "Posada" (house, dwelling, inn) in Hispanic countries. The custom is a "spiritual compensation" for the innkeeper's refusal to invite the Holy Family into his inn. Depending on the various cultures, the custom is practiced during Advent, sometimes from its beginning, sometimes starting with the feast of the Immaculate Conception, or—for the Posada—during the last week before Christmas. On Christmas, the statue or image of Our Lady (which was carried from home to home in procession and usually stayed for one or two days in each home) is returned to the church. This typical

Advent custom is practiced in different contexts, too. Special statues (Fatima, Our Lady of the Millennium, Pilgrim Mother Thrice Admirable) are carried from town to town, from parish to parish, from home to home to celebrate a special event or to pray for a special intention.

(See www.udayton.edu/Mary. For an example of Las Posadas, please enjoy the article in *The Lutheran*, December 1999, p. 31. You will find a summary online at: "Las Posadas," www.thelutheran.org/9912/page31.html. A wonderful telling is in the children's tale: *The Night of Las Posadas* by Tomie de Paola [Putnam Pub Group Juv, 1999]. A booklet with prayers and text for celebrating is *Las Posadas: A Bilingual Celebration for Christmas* by Kathryn J. Hermes, FSP, and Marlyn Monge [Pauline Books & Media, 2002].)

That somber reality, the purple of Advent, makes us pause. From crib to cross.

Again and again I need to be reminded that unlike the musical, *Jesus Christ Superstar*, which ends in death, Jesus' story does not end at the cross. This child put an end to death. All he asks is that I keep his word, and like Mary and Joseph at the birth, bow down in adoration.

Act

Is there a breach in a relationship? Can you put an end to wrath; turn your heart back to someone who hurt you?

Pray

Lord, let your glory dawn to take away our darkness.
May we be revealed as the children of light at the com-
ing of your Son.

(From the Opening Prayer of today's Mass)

Third Week of Advent

When the Church celebrates *the liturgy of Advent* each year, she makes present this ancient expectancy of the Messiah, for by sharing in the long preparation for the Savior's first coming, the faithful renew their ardent desire for his second coming.

(*Catechism of the Catholic Church*, nos. 523–524)

Sunday

of the Third Week of Advent

Ponder

THREE CANDLES ARE SUPPOSED to be glowing on the wreath, but where I worshipped this year the altar server couldn't light the third one. She quit trying, and in her rush to get to the procession on time, she tripped. We tried hard to contain our laughter. That's what this Sunday is all about.

Since the Vatican II reforms, the entire season of Advent now focuses on joy in anticipation of Jesus' coming. Long tradition, however, emphasized this Sunday as a special day of Christian joy. That is why, in some countries, a different-colored candle burns today. Our liturgy's entrance antiphon (usually omitted because we sing an opening hymn), is the text that gives rise to this Sunday's name, *Gaudete*, rejoice. *"Rejoice in the Lord always; again I will say, rejoice"* (Phil 4:4).

In an Angelus reflection, Pope John Paul II gives the reason for our joy:

To know that God is not distant but close, not indifferent but compassionate, not aloof but a merciful Father who follows us lovingly with respect for our freedom: all this is a cause of deep joy which the alternating ups and downs of daily life cannot touch.

An unmistakable feature of Christian joy is that it *can go hand in hand with suffering*, since it is based entirely on love. Indeed, the Lord who "is near," to the point of becoming man, comes to fill us with his joy, *the joy of loving*. Only in this way can we understand the serene joy of the martyrs even amid trial, or the smile of saints, full of charity for those who are suffering: a smile that does not offend but consoles.[5]

The season has reached its midpoint—like life. For the young, the midpoint of another school year has almost arrived—time enough to improve that final grade. For the elderly, who are well beyond life's midpoint, they may be thinking of another final grade, the day they meet the Lord face to face.

*M*ary, your journey comes very close to your delivery date. I wonder! As you traveled to Bethlehem, did you look at the faces of children on the way? What did you think? Did you pray for the children?

---

5. Pope John Paul II, *L'Osservatore Romano*, Angelus Message of December 14, 2003, English edition, n. 51/52, December 17/24 2003, p. 2.

At a shopping mall I sat on a bench not far from Santa where I could see the faces of the children. I decided to quietly finger my rosary under my shawl and make that my prayer time for the day. It wasn't long before I noticed that small children really do reflect the expressions of their parents. A tense-faced mom begets an uptight child. An impatient dad drags a whiny child with fear-filled face. But shiny adult eyes and strong, gentle movements gave rise to reflections in the faces of radiant children. Mary, did you make Jesus smile?

Act

Worship today! Take seriously the gathering of the churches to celebrate in Word and Eucharist—no matter what the tangled, knotted backside of the masterpiece called Church resembles.

Pray

"Holy Father, protect them in your name that you have given me, so that they may be one, as we are one. While I was with them, I protected them in your name that you have given me. I am not asking you to take them out of the world, but I ask you to protect them from the evil one" (Jn 17:11–12, 15).

Monday

of the Third Week of Advent

Ponder

A DELIGHTFUL CONTEMPORARY Christian song tells the tale of Balaam and his stubborn donkey. Balaam is hired to curse Israel, but the Lord sends an angel to instruct him in God's truth. Balaam doesn't see the angel, but the donkey does. In "donkey-terms" the donkey tries to let Balaam know about the angel. Balaam beats the donkey without seeking the reason for its behavior. After three beatings the donkey talks to Balaam. Finally Balaam learns how to see.

By listening to God, Balaam blesses Israel to the dismay of those who hired him. They grow angry, of course, but Balaam says: *"If Balak should give me his house full of silver and gold, I would not be able to go beyond the word of the LORD, to do either good or bad of my own will; what the LORD says, that is what I will say"* (Num 24:13).

Balaam's oracle announces the star that will come.

"I see him, but not now;
I behold him, but not near—
a star shall come out of Jacob,
and a scepter shall rise out of Israel..." (Num 24:17).

The earliest known image of the Blessed Virgin Mary with the child on her lap is a fresco found in the catacomb of Priscilla in Rome (early third century). A star shines above the dark-featured Madonna and Child, while to the left a man, probably Balaam, points to it. Anyone owning a *Catechism of the Catholic Church* can find the image in the beginning of the text. The authors placed it there to give us an example of what *Church* means. The Church comes

Christmas Novena

December 16 begins the novena of Christmas. Some families and religious institutions observe the custom of taking a statue of Mary from room to room nine days prior to Christmas. This is a form of shelter seeking. Family members take turns preparing a place for Mary and selecting stories, songs, and a reading to welcome her. A procession forms after supper beginning on December 15. During the following day, children are encouraged to visit Mary and wait for Jesus with her.

together to celebrate Christ. The Church longs for his coming and for his saving power. The Church is called to give birth to the Spirit of Jesus everywhere on this earth. Mary is the first to have given him birth and to have celebrated him. Indeed, Mary is the purest image of Church.

> By her complete adherence to the Father's will, to his Son's redemptive work, and to every prompting of the Holy Spirit, the Virgin Mary is the Church's model of faith and charity. Thus she is a "preeminent and...wholly unique member of the Church"; indeed, she is the "exemplary realization" (*typus*) of the Church (*Catechism of the Catholic Church*, no. 967).

"O" Antiphons

December 17 begins the final octave (eight days of intense prayer) before Christmas. The length of Advent varies, but the sequence is permanent from December 17 on.

If December 17 falls during this week, skip ahead to that reading.

Act

Today, ask Mary to teach you what it means to be Church, to have faith, and to practice charity. Ask her

what it meant for her to remain part of the first
Christian community with Peter and the disciples
gathered in the Upper Room. She stuck with the apostles and disciples who abandoned her son. Did she stay
for love of them, or for love of him?

Pray

"Righteous Father, the world does not know you, but I
know you; and these know that you have sent me. I
made your name known to them, and I will make it
known, so that the love with which you have loved me
may be in them, and I in them" (Jn 17:25–26).

Tuesday

of the Third Week of Advent

Ponder

SOMEONE ONCE LOOKED ME STRAIGHT in the eye and calmly said, "Do you realize your first response to my every question is *no*? Even reverse psychology doesn't work with you!"

In the Gospel chosen for today, Jesus poses a question about two sons. One is asked to do something, says he won't, but he thinks about it and does it. The other son says he will do it, but he doesn't. Which one did the Father's will?

His listeners give Jesus the right answer. Jesus then shocks us by telling us that those who apparently commit the worst sins are getting into heaven before we do. They ultimately listen to the Gospel challenges and turn themselves around. They know their need. They work with grace. We might be saying, *yes, yes, Lord*, but in reality do we let God-given opportunities slip away?

*M*ary, the wedding at Cana could so easily have been a place to let things slide. It wasn't your job; you were a guest. When you told them to do Jesus' bidding, what if the waiters had humored you a little, said, *yes, yes*, to you out of courtesy to a guest, but behind your back considered you to be an intruding busybody and then ignored you? An awful thought! They'd have missed the best wine! Mary, help my *yes* to be honest.

Act

Do as Mary did! Don't just sit there! Do something about the missing wine!

Pray

Father, prepare our hearts and remove the sadness that hinders us from feeling the joy and hope which his presence will bestow.

(From the *Roman Missal*)

Wednesday

of the Third Week of Advent

Ponder

MARY, HAVE YOU EVER been really angry—so angry that you lost it? We know that Jesus furiously reprimanded the money changers in the Temple. The authorities thought he lost it. But we believe that he knew precisely what he was doing and had to be drastic—that's different.

I lose it! All my attempted will power doesn't prevent the eruptions! They certainly aren't planned. It happens during my Christmas preparations, too. I want this to be such a special time of tender loving, to accompany you, to speak to the little Christ Child nearly ready to be born, and to do the Mary-like, Christ-like thing toward my family and neighbors. But, you know how it is.... My masterpiece gets tangled, its back side shows again and again.

*M*ary, you probably didn't lose it like I do, even if you felt frustrated at times. Your nature was in harmony. Use your influence to calm me down when my trip from Nazareth to Bethlehem gets too rough for me to handle.

An Advent Story

Frankie tossed and turned. He couldn't sleep. Finally he whispered, "God, are you there?" Frankie lay very still and listened with all his might.

"I'm here," said God.

"I have a problem," Frankie said. "God, you love everybody, don't you?"

"Yes, I love everyone."

"Do you love Lisa? She lives down the block."

"Yes, I also love Lisa who lives down the block," God replied.

"I usually like her a lot, too, but today I can't stand her," Frankie grumbled. "I get mad just thinking about her! Today, she messed up play practice just because she knew all her angel words and we didn't know our shepherd words. She said we should be sheep instead and just say *bah*. Worse yet, we should be trees and just stand there. I got so mad, I told her, 'What a scary, ugly angel you are!' We were both furious. I can't stand her now! I don't even *want* to like her anymore."

God asked, "You don't even *want* to like her?"

"Not even that!" Frankie whispered. Then he thought for a while. "God, can I make a wish? Tonight could you love Lisa twice as much because I can't do it? Please?"

"O, yes, I can do that," God said.

Frankie whispered, "Thank you! With all my heart thank you!" He turned over and fell sound asleep before he even had time to tell God good night.

(German original, author unknown)

Act

Christmas festivities, potlucks, and charities drain the pocket and amplify the strain. Nice on the street but nasty at home? Keep the focus and renew the priorities.

Pray

God, can I make a wish? Tonight could you love "Lisa" twice as much because I can't do it? Please?

Thursday

of the Third Week of Advent

Ponder

ISAIAH SPEAKS TO US AGAIN as he prepares us for the coming of the Lord. He uses images of women—those who are abandoned, barren, desolate, widowed, disgraced. Israel is compared to a woman who is utterly helpless under these circumstances.

It wasn't long ago that a television special focused on the deaths of some fifty addicted women on the North American continent who had been brutalized, beaten, and killed. Their remains were buried in the barnyard of a pig farm. The anchor and camera crew doing the special were approached by a desperate young woman at a stop sign who reached into the car begging for relief from her plight.

Hundreds of miles away, I was numbed by the horror of it all—in our time, in our sophisticated age—and there was nothing I could do, nothing at all I could do, except mourn the loss of this very young woman's beautiful feminine dignity. "Father," I prayed, "isn't there *something* that can change all this?"

Then I read Isaiah again, and Isaiah consoled me. Our gracious God does not forget.

> *Do not fear, for you will not be ashamed;*
> > *do not be discouraged, for you will not suffer disgrace;*
> *for you will forget the shame of your youth,*
> > *and the disgrace of your widowhood*
> > > *you will remember no more.*

> *For a brief moment I abandoned you,*
> > *but with great compassion I will gather you.*
> *In overflowing wrath for a moment*
> > *I hid my face from you,*
> *but with everlasting love I will have compassion on you*
> > *(54:4, 7—8).*

Act

Today, think of Mary, a widow, a desolate and disgraced mother of an executed criminal! Scripture tells us that this woman "stood" at the cross. She stood! Not as films depict her with loud wails and lamentation, but in the deeper pain of helpless sorrow and steadfast love. She stood there in the face of utter rejection.

At times, words fail us. We stammer clichés—even this sentence is a cliché—when our quiet, firm, and steadfast presence may offer the real consolation. The look on our face will tell those who suffer that we care—care intensely. The courage needed may be for ourselves—to look deeply into the eyes of those who are desolate and disgraced with calm and peaceful reassurance: I am here. I care.

Entrust to Mary, the Woman of Sorrows, those you know who share that destiny. Console them in your own way.

Pray

We fly to your patronage, O holy Mother of God; despise not our petitions in our necessities, but deliver us always from all dangers, O glorious and blessed Virgin.

(*Sub tuum*, third-century Egyptian papyrus)

Friday

of the Third Week of Advent

Ponder

JESUS DESCRIBES JOHN THE BAPTIST: *"He was a burning and shining lamp, and you were willing to rejoice for a while in his light"* (Jn 5:35).

Imagine if Jesus would describe you like that! Think of a *burning and shining lamp* on a dark, lonely road on a snowy night! I often have this image when I think of Joseph at the manger. He stands there quietly, lighted lamp in hand, offering welcome and shelter, his big brown cape surrounding his little family. I am indeed willing to *rejoice for a while in his light.*

How beautiful it would be if there were millions of men and women like Joseph who assume responsibility and remain steadfastly, strongly, silently committed to the vows they have taken and promises they have made. Words once said are forever. How ashamed I can be when I remember a

Saint Joseph and the Miracle Staircase

In Sante Fe the Sisters of Loretto had a chapel built. Unbelievably, no stairway access was built to the choir loft, and the architect died before he could add it. The Sisters prayed a novena to Saint Joseph for help. The day after they finished the novena, an elderly man with a toolbox, riding on a donkey, mysteriously arrived in town and asked if he could build the staircase. As the story is told, "The Church is cautious about spreading rumors of supernatural intervention, but the Sisters know that the miracle staircase is an answer to their novena to Saint Joseph. Some even think the gray-haired man on the donkey was Saint Joseph himself."

(Excerpt from *www.funtripslive.com/santa_fe/miracle_staircase/staircase.htm*)

promise I've made, but haven't kept. Quiet service might have been a brighter light.

When I'm really relaxed with others, I most cherish the moments of an easy togetherness in quiet. Rests in a musical score are as essential to the music as sound. When Christmas priorities are set, part of my weaving has threads of quiet time—especially quiet adoration *together with others* in the glow of the burning lamp at the crèche.

Act

*Renew the intention to spend quiet time resting in the
presence of the Lord. Be a light and safe haven for others.*

Pray

*Father, you entrusted our Savior to the care of
Saint Joseph. By the help of his prayers may your
Church continue to serve its Lord, Jesus Christ, who
lives and reigns with you and the Holy Spirit, one
God, for ever and ever.*

(From the Opening Prayer of the Mass of Saint Joseph)

Fourth Week of Advent

The Annunciation to Mary inaugurates "the fullness of time" (Gal 4:4), the time of the fulfillment of God's promises and preparations. Mary was invited to conceive him in whom the "whole fullness of deity" would dwell "bodily" (Col 2:9). The divine response to her question, "How can this be, since I know not man?" was given by the power of the Spirit: "The Holy Spirit will come upon you" (Lk 1:34–35).

(*Catechism of the Catholic Church*, no. 484)

Sunday
of the Fourth Week of Advent

Ponder

FOUR CANDLES BURN SUCCESSFULLY on the wreath.
True, our candles are lopsided and definitely not picture-
perfect. This is the third year we recycled the stubs.

This is the Sunday of school pageants, company dinners, packing late-shipment gifts, writing cards to those I
was going to drop from my list. After all, we haven't seen
each other for twenty-three years. Still, I was thrilled to
receive their personal note!

Getting to church today was quite a chore. Yet the liturgy turned closer to home, or so it seemed. Until now, the
Scriptures consistently pointed out that Advent concerns
the end of time when Jesus will come again. We are to listen
to John's advice and live our lives in such a way as to rejoice
in that final glorious day. As mysteriously beautiful and

comforting as that message is, what really warms my heart is the child in the manger.

The Chosen People had awaited the sovereign Lord and powerful king who would come to rule the nations. But a baby in a barn? This truly is the back side of things!

✦ ✸ ✦

Mary, the Gospel readings alternate about Joseph's dream, your Annunciation, and your visit to Elizabeth. All three of you believed in the wonderful thing about to happen. All three of you reacted differently. None of you could possibly have imagined how tangled and knotted your interwoven destiny would be with this little King of love born in Bethlehem, truly God, truly man.

Mary, your *faith* is the remarkable thing! It's God's gift to you, but also your gift in return. Please, Mary, would you share your faith with me?

Act

Today, take time to reflect on the second Advent preface below. Examine its tender message in the light of what this season has brought and will forever mean to you.

Pray

Father, all-powerful and ever-living God,
we do well always and everywhere to give you thanks
through Jesus Christ our Lord.

His future coming was proclaimed by all the prophets.
The virgin mother bore him in her womb
with love beyond all telling.
John the Baptist was his herald
and made him known when at last he came.

In his love Christ has filled us with joy
as we prepare to celebrate his birth,
so that when he comes he may find us watching in
*   prayer,*
our hearts filled with wonder and praise.

And so, with all the choirs of angels in heaven
we proclaim your glory
and join in their unending hymn of praise.

Christmas Vacation

Are children and grandchildren, nieces and nephews part of your Christmas festivities? Do you wonder how to keep them in the spirit of the season and focused on Jesus?

If you have a computer you can find projects and stories online that keep kids glued— even kids like me. Check my favorite first: *www.daughtersofstpaul.com/catholicchristmas*

December 17

Weekday of Advent

Ponder

O WISDOM ETERNAL,
proceeding from the mouth of the Most High,
you reach from end to end and
order all things mightily and sweetly;
come now to direct us in the way of holy prudence.

Manuscripts dating from the ninth and eleventh centuries show that a devotion known as the singing of the "O" *Antiphons* had been added to evening prayer in cathedral communities and monasteries from December 17 till Christmas Eve. Antiphons are brief chants or hymns sung before and/or after Psalms or biblical texts such as Mary's song, the *Magnificat.* The "O" expresses the profound longing of the human heart for the Savior.

The titles given to the coming Savior are taken from the Old Testament. The first letter of the seven key words in each antiphon (for example, Emmanuel) form an acrostic, *"ero cras,"* that means, "I will be tomorrow," a reference to Christ's imminent coming on Christmas.

Most Christians recognize the haunting melody of the Advent hymn, "O Come, O Come, Emmanuel." The verses of this hymn are one example of *"O" Antiphon* prayer.

> *O come, Thou Wisdom from on high, Who ord'rest*
> *all things mightily; To us the path of knowledge show,*
> *And teach us in her ways to go. Rejoice! Rejoice!*
> *Emmanuel Shall come to thee, O Israel!*

Dan Schutte has given expression to the same with his hymn, "Christ, Circle Round Us."

> Come, O Word of Truth, font of knowledge from on high.
> Come, Holy Wisdom, be our faithful friend and guide.
> Christ, circle round us. Christ, may your light surround us.
> Shine in our living. Fill our hearts with great thanksgiving.[6]

→ ※ ←

*M*ary, do you enjoy Ephraim the Syrian's poetry (second century) like I do? He speaks of wisdom like the *"O" Antiphons* do: *The High One became as a little child, and in*

---

6. Dan Schutte, "Christ, Circle Round Us," Oregon Catholic Press.

him was hidden a treasure of wisdom sufficing for all! Ephraim honors you with words he believes you would say:

> The day that Gabriel came in unto my low estate, he made me free instead of a handmaid, of a sudden: for I was the handmaid of thy Divine Nature, and am also the Mother of thy human Nature, O Lord and Son! Of a sudden the handmaid became the King's daughter in thee, thou Son of the King.... She wove for him and clothed him because he had put off his glory. She measured him and wove for him, since he had made himself little.[7]

Mary, you gave life to him who gave you life; you gave milk to him who gave you milk, and all that you are and have. He who was in the womb, opened wombs.

Act

Today, talk with Mary about knowledge and wisdom. With the explosion of knowledge today, ask her to help you sort out the important things to know.

Pray

Come, Holy Wisdom, be our faithful friend and guide. Christ, circle round us. Christ, may your light surround us. Shine in our living. Fill our hearts with great thanksgiving.

---

7. Ephraim the Syrian, *Nineteen Hymns on the Nativity of Christ in the Flesh.* (Translated: I. — XIII. by Rev. J. B. Morris, M.A. [Oxford Library of the Fathers]; XIV. — XIX. by Rev. A. Edward Johnston, B.D.).

December 18

Weekday of Advent

Ponder

O Lord and leader of the house of Israel,
who once appeared to Moses and
spoke to him from a bush aflame,
and on the peak of Sinai gave him the law;
come now, bring us your redemption
with your mighty outstretched arm.

Leaders and laws! We elect or vote on them, honor or dishonor them, keep them or break them—both leaders and laws. Why do we find those ancient ten laws, the commandments, so hard to take? Why do we expect to see in our leaders the face of *what is right* and decry what errs, but—in time—also find them hard to take, right or wrong?

At one time Israel was governed by judges, not kings. The people begged God for a leader who would guide them to prominence and peace. God heard the request, but

Saint Jerome's Christmas

Saint Jerome spent the last years of his life in Bethlehem, where he arrived on a Christmas day. Happy to be in the holy place on this day, he hurried to the crib to adore the holy Child at the very place of his nativity.

Saint Jerome saw the Christ Child in the poor little stable, lying on straw, just as Jerome always thought he would lie. Jerome fell on his knees, and prayed and meditated for a long time. Overcome with joy, he finally asked the child, "What can I give you? I give you all my possessions."

"Yes," said the Child, "but I want more."

"What else do you want? I give you my body, my intellect, my knowledge, all the books I wrote.... Can I give you more, holy Child?"

"Yes, Jerome, I want more of you."

After thinking a while, Jerome continued, "Holy Child, I give you my heart, a heart glowing with love for you. But this is all I have. I kept nothing for myself."

"Thank you," said the Christ Child. "You still did not give me all."

"Child, what can I give you?"

"I want your sins, your misery, your weakness. To take them away from humankind, I became a child."

through the prophets also warned the people: Only God is their true leader. Only God determines the norm for right and wrong.

But we can only know it through his Word. Without revelation, without the Word of God slowly revealed in time, no norms would exist.

When I break those commandments, I always make myself miserable, but I do it anyway—mostly in the name of love. That's just the question: Who defines the greatest gifts and who do I really love?

This ancient legend of Saint Jerome, translator of the Bible, comforts me:

Act

Give the holy Child your sins, your misery, your weakness. Acknowledge these things and walk humbly.

Pray

Holy Child, I give you my heart, a heart glowing with love for you.

(Saint Jerome)

December 19

Weekday of Advent

Ponder

O ROOT OF JESSE,
standing an ensign of the people,
before whom even kings silent will remain,
whom the Gentiles, too, shall beseech,
come now to deliver us all; delay no longer.

At the beginning of Advent, we may have made a Jesse tree and forced cherry blossoms to bloom to decorate our crèche. These are all *signs, symbols* made with our hands to honor and to love the baby in the manger. Jesus is the *one sign* of God's love manifest for his people.

In today's liturgy, Zechariah, husband of Elizabeth, cousin of Mary, has a hard time accepting and believing in love. Gabriel, the angel, tells Zechariah, *"I have been sent to speak to you and to bring you this good news. But now, because*

The Legend of the Poinsettia

Many years ago in a certain village in Mexico, the people would take gifts to the church and place them before the crèche on Christmas Eve. One evening a small boy stood outside the church door. With all his heart he wished he could enter the church and present a gift to Jesus, but he had nothing to give.

"I can at least pray," he thought. He knelt silently outside the church window and listened to the voices raised in song. When he rose to his feet again, he was amazed to see nearby a beautiful plant with scarlet leaves and a yellow flower in the center. He had never seen anything like it. He carefully plucked it, took it into the church, and placed the beautiful flower before the manger. He whispered, "This is my gift to the Christ Child. My own precious gift."

For a wonderful re-telling of this legend through a little girl's eyes, see *The Legend of the Poinsettia*, retold and illustrated by Tomie de Paola, 1994. See: *www.penguinputnam.com.*

you did not believe my words...you will become mute, unable to speak, until the day these things occur" (Lk 1:19–20). It took a long time for Zechariah to believe in his own power to once again love.

Mary, maybe that is why we like or hate Christmas. We believe or don't believe in the power of love, especially of God's redeeming love. Appearances of love and caring, without their real truth, like Zechariah, can become old, withered, silent. Scripture tells us that Zechariah went home to Elizabeth. He had the courage and God-given strength to take away her disgrace, to love again.

Does anyone have a right *not* to love? We make choices. Our definitions of love may differ, but as human beings we truly can make that choice.

Emerson, the poet, once wrote about Abraham Lincoln:

> [He] was at home and welcome with the humblest, and with a spirit and a practical vein in the times of terror that commanded the admiration of the wisest. His heart was as great as the world, but there was no room in it to hold the memory of a wrong.[8]

---

8. Emerson quoted in *One Thousand Beautiful Things*, compiled by Marjorie Barrows (Spencer Press, Inc., 1949).

In the end, Paul tells us in First Corinthians 13, we will be accountable for gifts entrusted to us at baptism: our faith, our hope, our love, and the greatest of these is love.

Act

It is time to ready your personal gift for the Christ Child. Rehearse today what birthday gift you have prepared for him. Be specific.

Pray

This is my gift to you, Christ Child. My own precious gift. Will it delight you?

December 20

Weekday of Advent

Ponder

O key of David, royal scepter of Israel,
you who open and no one closes;
who close and no one can open, come now,
and free humanity from its bonds in prison,
where it sits in darkness and the shadow of death.

One more day and the northern hemisphere will celebrate its longest night. Tradition tells us that Jesus was born
"when half-spent was the night." The symbols of darkness and
night powerfully express the human experience of futility,
dryness, and the oppressive sense of being unloved both by
God and other human beings.

Oddly, when we experience these things, we may
think no one else does or ever has. How it surprises us to
hear that great saints like Teresa of Calcutta—loved by mil-

lions—shared these same feelings. Mother Teresa wrote to her spiritual director:

> There is so much contradiction in my soul, such deep longing for God, so deep that it is painful, a suffering continual—yet not wanted by God, repulsed, empty, no faith, no love, no zeal.... Heaven means nothing to me, it looks like an empty place.

Another time she could write:

> I have begun to love my darkness for I believe now that it is a part, a very small part, of Jesus' darkness and pain on earth.

And:

> The whole time smiling—Sisters and people pass such remarks—they think my faith, trust, and love are filling my very being.... Could they but know—and how my cheerfulness is the cloak by which I cover the emptiness and misery.[9]

During his time in the United States, Father Joseph Kentenich, founder of the Marian apostolic movement, *Schoenstatt*, spoke in several Sunday sermons about the *divine smile* and *human cry*. As many authors through history, he referred to life as a game of love. God is the main player in this game. Kentenich knew—and spoke from experience—that "if God enlightens our minds so that we see the divine plan as a plan of love, a plan which guides our lives and convinces us that everything done, decreed, permitted

---

9. Mother Teresa of Calcutta quoted and translated by ZENIT December 15, 2003 (ZE03121524). Used with permission.

by God is an expression of love" then we will have mastered life, even if tears flow and darkness prevails.

> It is understood that my eyes, my lips reflect a joyful smile. I belong to God, I go continuously to God, I am carried by God, even when my eyes are filled with tears. A strong divine reflection still comes through, at least a little—the fruit of the awareness: God in me, God through me, all for him. This is the divine smile, this will be the eternal smile.[10]

Act

Will others see your good works and give you credit?
Do you think that your life—no matter how you try—
remains in oppressive darkness and your kindnesses
come from an empty heart? Today, ask Mary to share
her smile with you as you share yours with others.

Pray

Jesus, teach me to love my darkness for I believe now
that it is a part, a very small part, of your darkness
and pain on earth.

(Mother Teresa)

---

10. Joseph Kentenich, *The Game of Love*, Sermons, Book 2, p. 9. Printed as a manuscript by Schoenstatt Sisters of Mary, Waukesha, WI.

December 21

Weekday of Advent

Ponder

O Emmanuel, our ruler and lawgiver,
the expected of the nations and
the Redeemer of all,
come now to deliver us,
O our Lord and our master.

Emmanuel means *God with us.* The Gospel today tells
the story of Mary hurrying to help Elizabeth. She bears
Christ within her. No one on earth could say *God with us*
like Mary. Emmanuel within her makes hearts leap for joy.

Various paintings from the Middle Ages depict the
meeting of Elizabeth and Mary as an encounter of adoration. The older woman kneels before the younger, who in
turn insists that Elizabeth get up again. An old woman and
the child in her womb first adored Christ and knelt before
him, the Christ hidden in Mary's womb.

A Letter from a Friend in Rome, 2002

Now allow me to tell you a little about the city's celebration of Christmas. In general, the external surroundings in Rome don't remind  me much of Christmas. There is hardly any Christmas decoration anywhere. Nevertheless, a few signs point very definitely to Christmas. All the stores and stands sell Christmas items, a minimum of the usual ones like in the States, but a maximum of crib sets of various kinds....

I marveled on our Christmas journey to a few Roman churches to see the cribs and to pray to our new-born Savior-King. There were no Christmas trees in the churches, but two very important signs: Baby Jesus and the crib. A life-size figure of Baby Jesus was placed before the altar with special decorations all around. People were invited to come and do homage to Baby Jesus in their own way. On one of the side altars there is a huge manger scene with the stable placed into a life scene of either a country landscape of hills and valleys or of the city of Rome itself. We found some of the Roman sectors with their *piazzas*, their old buildings, and little narrow streets represented in a very real way.

> One of my deepest Christmas experiences was a pilgrimage to the basilica of Saint Mary Major, the oldest and largest Marian church. It is actually a Christmas church because in the crypt below the altar is enshrined the relic of the manger where Jesus was laid. To walk down the stairs, to kneel before this precious relic on the day when we celebrate the birth of Jesus is a special gift. On the opposite wall, in a cave-like setting, one finds the manger scene with its awe inspiring figures. All year round, this stable of Bethlehem, the foundation and heart of the basilica, proclaims the eloquent message of the crib to all those who listen: the glory of God in the lowliness of the child.
>
> (Personal letter to the author from Sr. M. Thomasine Treese.)

We can still give the Christ Child the gift of adoration, especially in this season of abundance. As the *Catechism of the Catholic Church* expresses it:

> To adore God is to acknowledge, in respect and absolute submission, the "nothingness of the creature" who would not exist but for God. To adore God is to praise and exalt him and to humble oneself, as Mary did in the *Magnificat*, confessing with gratitude that he has done great things and holy is his name. The worship of the one God sets man free from turning in on himself, from the slavery of sin and the idolatry of the world (no. 2097).

Act

Today, take quiet time to adore Christ. You can choose from many ways. As God, he is to be adored every-where, even in the stillness of our own souls. In our churches adore his presence in the Eucharist. At the crèche adore the child in the arms of his mother.

Pray

Come, Lord Jesus, come! Make your dwelling within me! Now and again let your presence be felt—by me and through me, in spite of me and because of me.

December 22

Weekday of Advent

Ponder

O KING OF ALL NATIONS,
the one for whom they have been yearning,
the cornerstone who unites all of them in perfect
    union,
come now, and rescue poor humanity,
which from dust you have fashioned.

The Church offers us the opportunity to gather together daily in prayer at the Eucharistic liturgy and the Liturgy
of the Hours. For centuries Christians have broken up the
day and night into periods of prayer, rest, work, and, yes,
recreation.

Through these meditations we have tried to ponder and
to pray, but what is prayer? Can I define what prayer is for
you? No one else's words fit right in our mouths or in our

patterns of thought. Each of us needs to speak to God in our own language, in our own way. Even so,

> Prayer cannot be reduced to the spontaneous outpouring of interior impulse: in order to pray, one must have the will to pray. Nor is it enough to know what the Scriptures reveal about prayer: one must also learn how to pray. Through a living transmission (Sacred Tradition) within *"the believing and praying Church,"* the Holy Spirit teaches the child of God how to pray (*Catechism of the Catholic Church*, no. 2650, emphasis added).

The *Catechism* goes on to tell us that "the Holy Spirit is the *living water* 'welling up to eternal life' (Jn 4:14) in the heart that prays." Christ is the source of the living water. "Indeed in the Christian life there are several wellsprings where Christ awaits us to enable us to drink of the Holy Spirit" (CCC, no. 2652). The Word of God and the liturgy of the Church are the main rich wellsprings.

Our life and work styles may make it difficult to participate in daily liturgy. What a gift for those who are able! They hear Jesus' teachings and receive his very flesh to be one with him. Even so, all the more, we need to make the commute to work and the marketplace the table of sacrifice and prayer. We need to find his face in those around us.

Spiritual writers tell us that images either reinforce concentration on prayer or distract from prayer. Some Eastern religions are noted for trying to reach a state of reflection that is uninterrupted by images. In the Western way of thinking, images can symbolize realities beyond themselves. In today's world of communication technology, images play a key role across all boundaries. To distill them from our senses isn't likely. Instead, we need to try to pass the images through a type of spiritual sieve so that they become part of our prayer.

Act

The keystone is Jesus Christ. He is our focus, our lens—our sieve. What would Jesus do if he saw what we see, heard what we hear, touched what we touch? Are we quiet enough to know?

Pray

"My soul magnifies the Lord, and my spirit rejoices in God my Savior, for he has looked with favor on the lowliness of his servant" (Lk 1:46).

December 23

Weekday of Advent

Ponder

A LITTLE CHILD IS BORN FOR US,
and he shall be called the mighty God;
every race on earth shall be blessed in him.

(Entrance Antiphon for December 23)

Once again today, as so often during Advent, the readings teach us about John and the mercy shown his parents. We hear the things that the Redeemer will do for his people. We wonder if these promises have been kept, or are they still to come? Have any of us *ever* been worthy of them?

It's like the promises I made at the beginning of this holy season. Have I kept them—at least some of them? Will I *ever* keep them? Or are they the kind of promises that need daily renewal?

A wonderful story is told of a little princess who shatters the crown of promise. Whose fault is it? The servant

who put the crown's stand too close, the carpenter who
built the wobbly stand, the poorly made container? Was it
just an accident or her own carelessness? Only when she
can say, "Daddy, it's my fault!" can the child find peace and
the merciful embrace of her father. But her father is utterly
good; he shows her how to take each shattered piece and
give it to him with love and deeds of kindness so the master
craftsman can make an even more precious crown.

Joseph is knocking; Mary is waiting. Whatever we
still have to do, only the heart matters.

Act

"He called a child, whom he put among them, and said,
'Truly I tell you, unless you change and become like
children, you will never enter the kingdom of heaven.
Whoever becomes humble like this child is the greatest
in the kingdom of heaven. Whoever welcomes one such
child in my name welcomes me'" (Mt 18:2–5).

Pray

Lord, as you nourish us with the bread of life, give
peace to our spirits and prepare us to welcome your
Son with ardent faith.

(From the Prayer after Communion of today's Mass)

A Children's Carol

When the eyes are sleeping,
but the soul is light,
Goes the Blessed Mother
through the winter night.

Knocks with tender speaking
at the door so mild:
Will you give me a present
for my Baby Child?

He will lie in the stable
suff'ring cold and harm,
Give him all your love,
love makes him warm.

Give him all your longing,
and the stall will be bright,
Kneel humbly adoring,
thus off'ring him light.

And open your heart
as crib for him wide,
He will work the wonder
of the Holy Night.

(German, source unknown)

December 24

Weekday of Advent

Ponder

O RADIANT DAWN,
splendor of eternal light and bright sun of justice,
come now and enlighten those
who sit in darkness and in the shadow of death.

Mary, at the midnight hour, you gave birth to God. It is time now to take your baby boy in your arms and gaze at his little face. God within you is now cradled in your arms, nursed, and tended by your love swelling beyond all telling.

New mothers weep and laugh all at once. Can anyone do a greater work on this earth than to bring forth life? Can anyone have a greater joy than yours, you who brought forth the truth, the way, and *the life*?

Joseph stands by you, and the Gospels hint that he alone helped you, since no one else gave you refuge. Yes, some paintings show your Joseph asleep with his back turned to the manger. This means that the child was not his. But Joseph *was* there and he could adore the child with all the love that fatherly care can lavish.

For a while, a brief and precious while, you and Joseph could be alone with your God in this wondrous hour. Did ox and ass sing and bend their knees? Were the angels waiting to see the human face of God?

Mary, the stable door opens softly as one by one the visitors begin to gather at the crèche. Here my journey ends. Here I long to stay! Here, come what may, I give my heart to your little King of Love.

Today, the Gospel is read that the Church prays every morning in her morning prayer for the Liturgy of the Hours. Zechariah, father of John, who could not speak until he named his child, spoke this prophetic canticle we call the *Benedictus*.

Act

God calls each of us to be a John, a child marked out to be the Lord's prophet. Each of our voices must praise him.

Pray

Blessed be the Lord God of Israel,
     for he has looked favorably on his people
        and redeemed them.
He has raised up a mighty savior for us
     in the house of his servant David,
as he spoke through the mouth of his holy prophets
     from of old,
that we would be saved from our enemies and from the
     hand of all who hate us.
Thus he has shown the mercy
     promised to our ancestors,
     and has remembered his holy covenant,
the oath that he swore to our ancestor Abraham,
to grant us that we, being rescued from the hands
        of our enemies,
might serve him without fear,
     in holiness and righteousness before him all our days.
And you, child, will be called the prophet
     of the Most High;
for you will go before the Lord to prepare his ways,
     to give knowledge of salvation to his people
        by the forgiveness of their sins.

By the tender mercy of our God,
the dawn from on high
will break upon us,
to give light to those who sit in darkness
and in the shadow of death,
to guide our feet into the way of peace.

(Lk 1:68–79)

Marian Feastdays in the Advent Season

December 8

The Immaculate Conception

DECEMBER 8 IS THE SOLEMNITY of the Immaculate Conception and a holy day of obligation. It is the patronal feast and solemnity for the United States and other countries entrusted to Mary's loving care.

December 8 is nine months prior to the Church's celebration of Mary's birthday on September 8. Due to Mary's role in salvation history, we remember that she was conceived in the natural way of human relations, and, at that moment, we believe God made her a new creation, like Adam and Eve before the fall, free for her whole life of the tendencies to sin, that is, to turn away from God. The Creator gave Mary this gift for the sake of his Son, that the vessel who carried him in her womb, nursed him, educated him, and cared for him would be a human being fully in harmony with God, within herself, and in all her relationships to the rest of creation.

Is Mary simply a vessel with no real choice of her own? Look at Adam and Eve; they walked with God, but, faced with their freedom, they turned from him. In her freedom Mary embraced him, conceiving him in her faith before giving him a home among us in her womb.

What does this have to do with us? Freedom from sin is the promise of our baptism into Christ. Our adoption as children of God frees us from this inheritance. In her earthly life, Mary anticipated what human life in God was and is meant to be. With us, there is one difference: from the womb the divine potter has allowed our vessel to be fragile and flawed. Though healed, we were once broken. We will always have the tendency to break, to turn away by our own free will.

December 12

Our Lady of Guadalupe, Patroness of the Americas

When Mary appeared to Juan Diego, the Aztecs were still performing human sacrifices. Within ten years after the appearance, nine million had been baptized, and human sacrifices had ended.

Through the centuries Mary has visited the simple, the little ones, the poor. In a gentle voice and in the looks and languages of the people, she calls for prayer and conversion. Mainly, she calls for love. True love wants to see the beloved face to face. Mary was permitted to do that like no other. She was Jesus' first home on earth. She wants us to give him a home, too, wherever we are.

Juan Diego's tilma shows an image of a woman with child. Mary's whole purpose is to know Jesus, love him, serve him, and, yes, to bring him to us.

We call Mary the Star of Evangelization—like the ancient Christmas star, she leads the shepherds, the wise, the childlike to her beloved divine and human Son. Mary comes to teach us the prayer of Jesus: thy kingdom come; thy will be done *on earth*...

Marian Advent Festival

Everyone can contribute to the celebration of Christmas in some unique, original way. Are you a member of a parish? Single? Married? Widow or widower? Perhaps you would like to help initiate a warm stream of Christmas love and celebration in honor of Mary. One way might be to suggest to your pastor or someone on your parish council to begin to honor her with a Marian Advent festival.

Wouldn't it be wonderful if throughout North America, December 8–12 became five days of festive parish celebration? Framed in the liturgies of the Immaculata and Guadalupana, plan ways for your parish to welcome a celebration of the Incarnation in a Marian way:

> *Walk with the pre-redeemed Mary (woman of faith who welcomes Christ and lives life in simplicity and constant giving);*

> *Walk with the pregnant Mary (foster respect for life and the dignity of motherhood);*

> *Walk with the Mary who hurries to serve Elizabeth (visit shut-ins, respect and love the elderly);*

> *Walk with Mary who journeys to Bethlehem with Joseph (foster respect for men, laborers, fathers of families).*

For numerous things Marian: knowledge, devotional practices, art, music, homily helps, meditations, poetry, and more, see The Mary Page, www.udayton.edu/Mary.

Saints in the Advent Season

December 3

Francis Xavier (1506–1552)

Francis' feast may not always fall directly in Advent, but when it does, he gives us an Advent example of what love and commitment can do. He was one of the six men who, with Ignatius of Loyola, founded the Society of Jesus, the Jesuits. The same year the Church recognized the order, Ignatius sent him to the Far East. His Advent message to us: Let nothing hinder you from telling the Good News of Jesus' coming—then and now.

December 4

John of Damascus (675–749)

Though the stories about John are mixed with legend and improbabilities, we remember him especially for two things: his poetry and his defense of images, which earned him the title "Doctor of Christian Art." Thanks to him, Christians continue to imagine through art the wonderful stories of redemption. What would Christmas be today without these myriad images!

December 6

Nicholas of Bari, Bishop (fourth century)

Patron of bakers and pawnbrokers, this good bishop, in all his derivations, represents the Christian prism of giving. In Germany, he comes on the eve of his feast day, checks his list of "naughty and nice," and takes a letter back to heaven to the Christ Child, the one who actually brings presents on Christmas.

> For a delightful and practical way to celebrate Nicholas as a family, see *Advent, Christmas and Epiphany in the Domestic Church*, by Catherine and Peter Fournier, www.Domestic-Church.com. Other good resources are *The True Story of Santa Claus* by Paul Prokop, and *How St. Nicholas Became Santa Claus* (video and book) by Bernie Marquis (both from Pauline Books & Media).

December 9

Juan Diego (1474–1548)

A weaver, farmer, and laborer, Juan Diego was also a family man. The story of Our Lady's visits to him with her gifts and requests is well known. For an English translation of the earliest known account written fourteen years after the event, see Mary Page at: www.udayton.edu/mary/meditations/guadalupe.html. This site contains homily helps, poetry, and further reflections on the significance of Our Lady of Guadalupe, who cares for the poor, the simple, the forgotten, and the conquered.

December 13

Lucy (third century)

Patron of the blind and those with eye problems, we have little authentic knowledge of Lucy, whose name means "light." Nevertheless, customs for Lucy's feast are popular from Scandinavia to Sicily. Perhaps best known is the wreath of lights she wore on her head to free her hands as she climbed down into the catacombs to bring food to Christians in hiding.

> For a recipe and more on customs, see *Advent, Christmas and Epiphany in the Domestic Church*, www.Domestic-Church.com.

Season of Christmas

Jesus was born in a humble stable, into a poor family. Simple shepherds were the first witnesses to this event. In this poverty heaven's glory was made manifest. The Church never tires of singing the glory of this night:

The Virgin today brings into the world the Eternal
And the earth offers a cave to the Inaccessible.
The angels and shepherds praise him
And the magi advance with the star,
For you are born for us,
Little Child, God eternal!

To become a child in relation to God is the condition for entering the kingdom. For this, we must humble ourselves and become little. Even more, to become "children of God" we must be "born from above" or "born of God" (Jn 3:7; 1:13; 1:12). Only when Christ is formed in us will the mystery of Christmas be fulfilled in us."

(*Catechism of the Catholic Church*, nos. 525–526)

Christmas Eve

Ponder

ACCORDING TO THE LITURGY, which remembers ancient Jewish ritual custom, a day is reckoned from sunset to sunset. Christmas Eve is truly Christmas with all the trimmings!

On this evening the youngest member of a family places the Christ Child in the manger, songs previously unsung resonate warmth, the fire burns, tree lights glow as does every candle on the mantle, in the window, and on the doorstep. In my family, we enjoy a simple yet special supper. When I was a child we opened one gift this night. After all, it was a long wait till Midnight Mass.

Times change, customs change. But, by all means celebrate!

If you are single and celebrate alone this night, perhaps a good book of Christmas stories will fill your soul with joy. Peter Vance Orullian has an interesting collection entitled *At the Manger: The Stories of Those Who Were There.* The stories at first seem stilted, rather awkwardly written, not always as our faith teaches. One is tempted to set the book down. Slowly, the stories weave together, and in the final story the Christmas Eve scene is fulfilled. "Other faces were familiar to me. Standing in their company, and all of us attendant to the beautiful child, I felt a quiet within, a sureness, I had never known...."[11] Weeks after reading the book, I recalled "those who were there" even if the sharing is silent.

Each of us, alone in our identity, alone in the singular, unique way we stand before the little King in the manger, nevertheless senses the inner bond of all who find their way to the crèche. Here we are together. We may never have spoken, perhaps we never will, but here in the dark shadows of the stable—and in the shadows of the pillars of our churches—we sense one another. We know we share a common destiny. Our little Lord has come to call all of us close to his heart and take us home one day, but he also would have come for just one of us. So, during this holy night, I quietly wish my neighbors well, for I know they love as I do.

Ours is a *universal* Church. We can be there for everyone by the *universality* of our intentions, even when we are alone. Prayer knows no distance or boundaries. Our focus is the newborn child in the manger. Our lens is to lay at his feet our lives, our intentions, our interests, our material

---

11. Peter V. Orullian, *At the Manger: The Stories of Those Who Were There* (Mill Creek, WA: Descant Publishing, 2001).

goods or lack of them, but especially whatever love we can muster.

Song of the Ship

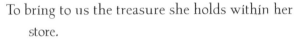

There comes a galley sailing
    with angels flying fast;
She bears a treasured cargo be-
    neath her mighty mast.
Upon the silent waters the ship
    glides into shore,
To bring to us the treasure she holds within her
    store.
For this ship's name is Mary, the fairest rose is she;
She brings us all her Baby whose love shall make
    us free.

(Johann Tauler, fourteenth century, *Andernacher Gesangbuch.*
Andernach is a small town along the Rhine River.)

Act

Celebrate! By all means celebrate! Most of all, cele-
brate with worship!

Pray

Mary, the hour of your delivery has come! Emmanuel
within you will now be Emmanuel in your arms, and

you will let us hold him for a while till he needs your warmth and nourishment again. Can any joy compare with the joy of his needing you? He who is Lord and King really made himself so small as to need you. Mary, when I'm holding him tonight, maybe he will show me, too, how he needs me. Allow me to be an instrument in his hand.

Christmas Day

Ponder

YOUR ETERNAL WORD LEAPED DOWN FROM HEAVEN
in the silent watches of the night,
and how your Church is filled with wonder
at the nearness of her God.

(Opening Prayer of the Mass at Dawn)

John Saward's *Redeemer in the Womb* reminds us that
our encounter with the Christ Child is indeed touchable.
He can really come and dwell within us. Saward writes:

The embryonic Christ, simply by being what he is, proclaims
in advance his later teaching: "Unless you change and
become like little children, you will never enter the kingdom
of heaven" (Mt 18:3). God took the "little way" when he
became man. He came and lay "all so still where his Mother
was." Without throwing off his divine grandeur, he took the
smallest form of human life.... He is the first realization of his
parable of the mustard seed (cf. Mt 13:31–32). The Father's
Word is sown by the Holy Spirit as a tiny grain of humanity

in the Virgin-field, and then, having reached the ripeness of manhood, having taught and healed, having suffered and died, he becomes in the Resurrection the mighty Tree of Life housing angels and men and all creation in his arms....

In the manner of his Incarnation, God exposes the folly of self-aggrandizement and proves the wisdom of humility. He could have assumed human nature in adult form and proceeded swiftly to his task, but he chose not to. He took the low road, the slow route of human growth from con-ception, blessing every staging-post on the highway. As Saint Irenaeus understood so well, patience is an attribute of God before it is a virtue of man.

The Holy Eucharist continues the little way of the Incarnation. The great God who became a baby in Mary's womb here gives his whole mighty self—Body, Blood, Soul, and Divinity—in the tiny form of the host. And he invites a Mary-like response of wholehearted welcome.[12]

Act

Welcome the child—and with him welcome everyone without exception.

Pray

Mary, according to Scripture there was no such thing as quiet revelry for you and Joseph and the Baby.

---

12. John Saward, *Redeemer in the Womb* (San Francisco: Ignatius Press, 1993), p. 161.

Angels sang and shepherds came. Probably the
innkeeper with all his guests and so many more! You
had to be there for them—and for him. Teach me,
Mary, how to be here—for them and for him.

O Come, Little Children

O come, little children, O
    come, one and all!
O come to the cradle in
    Bethlehem's stall!
Come, see what has happened
    this holiest night;
Come, gaze on the gift from the Father of Might.

O see where he's lying, the heavenly Boy!
Here Joseph and Mary behold him with joy;
The shepherds have come, and are kneeling in
    prayer,
While songs of the angels float over him there.

O come, join the shepherds, and on bended knee
Give thanks to the Father for Jesus, our King.
O lift up your voices and join in the praise,
That angels from heaven to the Father now raise.

(German, Christoph von Schmid, J. A. P. Schulz)

The Christmas Spirit

OUR CULTURE HAS A TENDENCY to end the season of Christmas early. Decorations have been up long before the big shopping Friday after Thanksgiving. Wind and weather begin to make things look a bit shabby. The work world continues, probably more concerned with New Year's Eve parties than the continuation of Christmas, whose theme may be getting old on the party circuit.

Nonetheless, we have on-going reason to celebrate. Each of the following carries through the joyful festival of our Lord's birth:

Holy Family of Jesus, Mary, and Joseph, Sunday
   between Christmas and New Year or December 30

Blessed Virgin Mary, Mother of God, January 1

World Day of Peace, January 1

Epiphany of the Lord, Sunday after January 1 (in some
   countries on January 6)

Baptism of the Lord, Sunday after January 6

Likely, we will not continue our ten-minute evening reflection in anticipation of each coming day. Now we enjoy the hour of fullness and completion. Now is the time to live what we have hoped for.

With children on vacation, family visits are a must. This is the time to break loneliness in any way the imagination can play. Old-fashioned ideas from fifty years ago or more might recycle into wonderful experiences if treated with wisdom, hot chocolate, and moderation. Visit the crèches in churches on the other side of town, find a Marian shrine in your area, stop by the home of elderly priests or sisters to remember the good years of their service. You'll know best how to bring Christ's love as Mary did. Your brief visit will be welcome if you come with blessings in your heart.

Holy Family of Jesus, Mary, and Joseph

Holy Family Sunday is a wonderful day for parents and children to dedicate a corner of their home to God with a little home altar. The Second Vatican Council talked about the domestic church. Church is and begins at home. A *place* set aside reminds us of that. In Germany, generations of Black Forest families called this the *Lord God's corner.* One found a cross there, a statue of Mary, the images of the Sacred Hearts of Jesus and Mary, and those mementos that held religious meaning for the family. The worldwide Marian movement,

Schoenstatt, has a similar practice called a home shrine, a little place of prayer where the crucifix and Marian image are set up and blessed. The home shrine needs to be accessible to the whole family on a permanent basis.

In this place, first graders can bring their coloring book pages to Mother Mary and Baby Jesus with good Saint Joseph looking on. Here, a young teen may place her first gift rose in joy and excitement—when no one is looking, of course. At this spot, a Mom turns with a quick prayer for her skateboarding son. Dad loves it, too. Make it a beautiful, but touchable place.

If one is alone, it is all the more important to invite the Holy Family home. Various spiritualities and movements enrich the Church by helping us deepen our committed Christian life at whatever stage it is. The Pauline Family (sharers in the spirit of Mary and the apostles, publishers of this book) and the Schoenstatt Movement (the author's source of inspiration and formation) are examples of new forms of life that seek to deepen the faith and Marian love for Christ. Church is not *out there somewhere*; Church is my life and my home with Jesus as its focus.

Blessed Virgin Mary, Mother of God and World Day of Peace

New Year's Day has such varied content—from the Rose Parade to a holy day of obligation. Today, thank Mary for accepting her part in salvation history, to bear God to us—then and now. Today we also celebrate World Day of Peace—promoted by the popes and entrusted to Mary. On this day, the Holy Father sends his papal blessing upon the whole world. Those who can witness this on television find rich inspiration and participate in the blessing.

Being God's Mother didn't make Mary divine. She had to struggle with all things human. Even with her nature in harmony and untouched by sin, she had to struggle in faith to fully recognize God's will. Father Kentenich, founder of the Schoenstatt Movement (1885–1968), wrote in Dachau:

> Immaculate Virgin, you struggle there in prayer,
> filled with longing for the dawn of salvation.
> There Gabriel speaks God's request
> and your Fiat illumines the world.[13]

Mary's divine maternity secures the identity of Jesus. He is God and Man. He is all the humanness that we are, except sin.

Blessed James Alberione, founder of the Pauline Family (1884–1971), looks at it another way:

> Why did he make Mary Mother of God
> and of the Church? So that she would be
> the Queen of the Apostles and the true Apostle.

---

13. Joseph Kentenich, *Heavenwards: Prayers Written in Dachau* (Waukesha, WI: Schoenstatt Press, 1992).

Hence, her very dignity as Mother of God
is in relation to her office as Apostle—
to give Jesus to the world,
to give him as the God-man,
and to give the Church
until the consummation of time,
because today Christ is the Church.
To listen to the Church is to listen to Jesus Christ.
Mary is the Apostle. Relative to us
she is Queen because she calls us
to participate in her apostolate;
because she is greater than all apostles;
and because she gathers and instructs all apostles.
To them she gives graces and prepares the reward
of glory.[14]

Epiphany of the Lord

When I was a child, Epiphany seemed to be like a post-script, a vague ending to Christmas, actually long over in our household. Why we celebrated it so long after New Year's seemed out of place. Our Christmas tree had long since been taken outside. It took a long time until I began to learn the liturgical meaning of Epiphany.

This is changing for an ever growing number of Americans. Our Hispanic cultures have brought us the fes-

---

14. *Mary Leads Us to Jesus: The Marian Spirituality of Blessed James Alberione, SSP,* edited by Marianne Lorraine Trouvé, FSP (Boston: Pauline Books & Media, 2004), pp. 14—15.

tivities of Three Kings. This day, not Christmas, is the main gift exchange day. Ethnic foods add to the celebration. Serenades for Baby Jesus with tambourines, maracas, drums, triangles, and guitars make every heart smile.

This is the manifestation of the Lord. *This* is the day kings bow before the Child in the crib, the Child in the arms of his Mother, the Child protected by strong Joseph. This is the day when fathers dress as kings and bring gifts to families of the poor. In some countries, like Germany, the young dress as the kings with a star pinned on a band around their foreheads or carrying a staff topped by a star. They go from door to door begging alms for the missions.

This is also the day when the kings, be they children or adults, write the letters of the year in chalk on the top of the door frame of the main entrance with the letters C+M+B. [For example: 20+C+M+B+06.] Some say these letters represent the traditional names given to the wise men: Caspar, Melchior, and Balthasar. More likely, the blessing is meant: *Christus mansionem benedicat* (May Christ bless this house).

Another Epiphany tradition enjoyed by all is the Christ Cake. A tiny plastic replica of Baby Jesus is baked into a cake. Fortunate the one who finds the Christ Child in his or her piece! Another custom in some areas is to make a cake with three beans baked into it. The cake is served the night before Epiphany. The persons finding the beans play the part of the kings on the following day.

The *piñata* made dear in our Mexican traditions has a far deeper meaning than known to many of us! Originally, the *piñata* was made in the shape of a seven-pointed star. The seven points represent the seven capital sins (pride, avarice, envy, wrath, lust, gluttony, and sloth or *acedía*; see *CCC*, no. 1866).

A person is blindfolded to represent that we are somehow blinded as we walk through life fighting against these vices that can destroy us. Someone places a staff into the person's hands. The staff represents the Church, which helps us to strike down the vices. Those who stand around waiting their turn sing, telling us not to miss the point:

> *Pegándole a la piñata*
> *los niños cantan:*
> *Dale, dale, dale,*
> *no pierdas el tino,*
> *porque si lo pierdes*
> *pierdes el camino.*
> *Dale, dale, dale,*
> *dale y no le dió,*
> *quítenle la venda*
> *porque sigo yo.*

The translation is:

While they hit the *piñata*
the children sing:

Hit it, hit it, hit it,
don't lose your orientation,
because if you lose it
you lose your way.
Hit it, hit it, hit it,
hit it and he didn't hit it,
remove from him the blindfold
because it is my turn.

Because of our wounded nature, we still can't see rightly, but with the help of the staff we can swing at the sins
more vigorously and, finally, victoriously experience the
sweet outpouring of grace represented by the sweets hidden in the *piñata.*

All the Way to the Baptism of the Lord

The days are still short, the nights long and dark.
Children, grandchildren, nieces, and nephews grow rest-
less. They can't stay out all day, nor can they be occupied
with *things* only. They need interaction and appropriate dialogue with loving adults. This might be the time—now in
the true Christmas season—to learn of customs from other
lands and possibly act them out in simple ways. For little
ones up to about eight years old, Susan Titus Osborn,
Christine Tangvald, and Jodie McCallum have teamed up
to publish a book depicting how children from ten countries celebrate Christmas: *Children Around the World*

Celebrate Christmas (Standard Publishing Co., 1996). It includes pages for a child to fill in how he or she celebrates Christmas. There are projects included in the back for a *piñata*, santons, paper chains, and Christmas pudding. For tiny children today there are countless read-to-me, touchable books. Children cherish these experiences.

For older children and childlike adults, Mary D. Lankford's *Christmas Around the World* (Harper Trophy, 1998), goes into greater detail on how twelve countries celebrate Christmas. Her book includes a useful Christmas chronology and celebration ideas from secular to religious. Illustrations by Karen Dugan also make this an attractive coffee table piece.

Ace Collins comes from a general Christian perspective with his *Stories Behind the Great Traditions of Christmas* (Zondervan, 2003). His research tells of angles we might never have known.

Tomie de Paola writes, illustrates, and revives customs in a way that makes one happy about our Catholic Christian culture. Examples are *The Night of Las Posadas* (Putnam Pub Group Juv, 1999) and *An Early American Christmas* (Holiday House, 1992).

If you are looking for a priceless and timeless Marian piece that will become a family treasure, think about obtaining *Mary: Art, Culture, and Religion through the Ages* (Crossroad / Herder & Herder, 1998). This translation from a team of German authors reflects Marian teachings and devotions through the ages.

For a wealth of ideas on how to celebrate with children, see *The Advent-Christmas Book: Living and Celebrating Our Catholic Customs and Traditions* by Joan Marie Arbogast (Pauline Books & Media, 2004).

Finally, you might also enjoy further reflections from this author in Vincenzina Krymow's *Mary's Flowers: Gardens, Legends & Meditations* (St. Anthony Messenger Press, 2002). Many legends associate flowers with the nativity and flight to Egypt.

An Advent well lived brings a Christmas season of wonder, light, love, and joy. Doesn't it remind us of Mary's Advent? After the angel's visit, Mary could have retreated to her room filled with the Son of God, given over to contemplation and wonder, protective of self and of the child within her. Not so! She hurried away to help her dear old cousin; she traveled with Joseph to Bethlehem—to ox and ass and a bed of dried grass. Mary's way balanced both adoration and service. Could we have it any better?

Together with the Church, we pray a Christmas Preface:

Father, all-powerful and ever-living God,
we do well always and everywhere to give you
thanks through Jesus Christ our Lord.

Today you fill our hearts with joy
as we recognize in Christ the revelation of your
  love.
No eye can see his glory as our God,
yet now he is seen as one like us.

Christ is your Son before all ages,
yet now he is born in time.
He has come to lift up all things to himself,
to restore unity to creation,
and to lead mankind from exile
into your heavenly kingdom.

With all the angels of heaven
we sing our joyful hymn of praise!

Saints in the Christmas Season

December 26

Stephen, First Martyr
(Acts 6:8–10; 7:54–59)

Stephen, full of grace and power, did great wonders and signs among the people... 'Look... I see the heavens opened and the Son of Man standing at the right hand of God.

The Liturgy of the Hours, in the response to the second reading, tells us why the Church celebrates Stephen the day after Christmas: "Yesterday the Lord was born on earth that Stephen might be born in heaven."

Some countries observe this second Christmas day as a national holiday; one day doesn't suffice to truly celebrate. In the British Commonwealth, this is Boxing Day, the day of gift-giving to thank persons of service, and to help those in need.

December 27

John, Apostle and Evangelist

John, Beloved Apostle of the Lord, is honored with his feast day so close to Christmas because of his strong, enduring love for Jesus. At Mass we hear the beginning of John's first letter. He writes:

> What we have heard, what we have seen with our eyes, what we have looked at and touched with our hands, concerning the word of life—this life was revealed...so that you also may have fellowship with us; and truly our fellowship is with the Father and with his Son Jesus Christ (1:1—3).

On Saint John's Day in some countries, people serve the best wine to celebrate John's great love for Jesus.

December 28

Holy Innocents, Martyrs (Mt 2:16—18)

The enigma of babies dying because of Jesus is incredibly difficult to explain, especially to children. How could anyone hate or fear the little King of Love in Bethlehem! Perhaps it is a very good thing that children are on Christmas break for Innocents' Day. No doubt! The first reading assures us that his precious Blood will have saved these innocents.

What of today's innocents? Little white crosses crammed together on a university campus green startled me one January day. Light snow dusted them. Hunkered down for the long haul, two students passed out tracts to pray for the unborn. The young man noted my unasked question. "These are the ones we couldn't save right here on our own campus," he said. "Their mothers are our classmates." Then he walked away. The young woman added, "Pray for me, too. I was one of them."

January 4

Elizabeth Ann Seton (1774–1821)

The first native-born American saint, Elizabeth's story is one of love, tragedy, and conversion. Six sisters' communities trace their origins to her initial foundation.

January 5

John Neumann (1811–1860)

Born in Bohemia, ordained in New York, John Neumann entered the Redemptorists and later became Bishop of Philadelphia. He was the first to organize a diocesan Catholic school system in the United States.

January 6

Blessed André Bessette (1845–1937)

Deeply devoted to Saint Joseph, Holy Cross Brother André Bessette established a shrine to him in Montreal. André is known for his simple, healing love and his sense of humor.

Acknowledgments

Sincere gratitude to M. Marcia Vinje and Joan Biemert for their critical review and encouragement of this manuscript.

Note About the Author

M. JEAN FRISK, S.T.L., is a member of the secular institute of the Schoenstatt Sisters of Mary (ISSM). She holds a licentiate in sacred theology from The Marian Library / International Marian Research Institute in Dayton, Ohio, where she collaborates as adjunct professor and contributes to the Mary Page (www.udayton.edu/mary). Her area of study is Mary in catechesis. She is a textbook consultant regarding Marian teachings, recognized for award winning writings, and has written the introductions to the Church documents on Mary in the collection *Mother of Christ, Mother of the Church* (Pauline Books & Media). She currently resides in Westfield, Massachusetts, where she helps to coordinate the Schoenstatt Movement, and continues to write "in the shadow of Mary's shrine."

BOOKS & MEDIA

The Daughters of St. Paul operate book and media centers at the following addresses. Visit, call or write the one nearest you today, or find us on the World Wide Web, www.pauline.org

CALIFORNIA

3908 Sepulveda Blvd, Culver City, CA 90230	310-397-8676
5945 Balboa Avenue, San Diego, CA 92111	858-565-9181
46 Geary Street, San Francisco, CA 94108	415-781-5180

FLORIDA

145 S.W. 107th Avenue, Miami, FL 33174	305-559-6715

HAWAII

1143 Bishop Street, Honolulu, HI 96813	808-521-2731
Neighbor Islands call:	800-259-8463

ILLINOIS

172 North Michigan Avenue, Chicago, IL 60601	312-346-4228

LOUISIANA

4403 Veterans Memorial Blvd, Metairie, LA 70006	504-887-7631

MASSACHUSETTS

885 Providence Hwy, Dedham, MA 02026	781-326-5385

MISSOURI

9804 Watson Road, St. Louis, MO 63126	314-965-3512

NEW JERSEY

561 U.S. Route 1, Wick Plaza, Edison, NJ 08817	732-572-1200

NEW YORK

150 East 52nd Street, New York, NY 10022	212-754-1110

PENNSYLVANIA

9171-A Roosevelt Blvd, Philadelphia, PA 19114	215-676-9494

SOUTH CAROLINA

243 King Street, Charleston, SC 29401	843-577-0175

TENNESSEE

4811 Poplar Avenue, Memphis, TN 38117	901-761-2987

TEXAS

114 Main Plaza, San Antonio, TX 78205	210-224-8101

VIRGINIA

1025 King Street, Alexandria, VA 22314	703-549-3806

CANADA

3022 Dufferin Street, Toronto, ON M6B 3T5	416-781-9131

¡También somos su fuente para libros, videos y música en español!